Nocturnal Witchcraft

The Mysteries of the Dark Await You

If you've picked up this book, you may just be one of those souls who walk an often-misunderstood spiritual path. You may be one of nightkind.

Traditional Wicca and other occult currents may have looked enticing at first, but could have left you feeling a bit alienated, as was the case with me. Most of these paths have evolved, through group input, to suit the greatest common denominator: to resonate with those who favor both solar and lunar energies.

Some of us live for the night, however. Some of us only feel a need for the light of the moon.

This book is for all of you who wish to follow the nocturnal path. I hope you'll find in the Craft of Night everything that you seek.

Imagine divining with the night and reading minds, or enhancing your personal magnetism and affecting how others perceive you. How about taking spellcasting to a level you thought only possible in fantasy novels? You will learn to alter reality in this book, as well as how to master contacting aspects of the unseen world in ways you never thought possible.

The Gods and Goddesses of Night await you in the pages that follow, as do other universal energies, some as misunderstood as perhaps you've felt yourself to be.

Be you nightkind or curious seeker, welcome. We're about to explore nocturnal mysteries that have never before been gathered in one place.

—Konstantinos

About the Author

Konstantinos has a bachelor's degree in Journalism and Technical Writing and is a published author of articles and short fiction. This is his fourth book published by Llewellyn. He is also the author of *Vampires: The Occult Truth*, *Summoning Spirits: The Art of Magical Evocation*, and *Contact the Other Side: 7 Methods for Afterlife Communication*.

A Dark Neopagan, Konstantinos has been researching the occult and practicing magick for over fifteen years. He is also a trained stage mentalist who uses these skills to debunk fraudulent affectations of the supernatural. Konstantinos often lectures on paranormal topics at bookstores and colleges. He also devotes time to singing Gothic rock music, and to exploring nocturnal life both in New York City and around the country.

To Write to the Author

If you wish to contact the author or would like more information about this book, please write to the author in care of Llewellyn Worldwide and we will forward your request. Both the author and publisher appreciate hearing from you and learning of your enjoyment of this book and how it has helped you. Llewellyn Worldwide cannot guarantee that every letter written to the author can be answered, but all will be forwarded. Please write to:

Konstantinos
℅ Llewellyn Worldwide
P.O. Box 64383, Dept. 0-7387-0166-1
St. Paul, MN 55164-0383, U.S.A.
Please enclose a self-addressed stamped envelope for reply,
or $1.00 to cover costs. If outside U.S.A., enclose
international postal reply coupon.

Many of Llewellyn's authors have websites with additional information and resources. For more information, please visit our website at http://www.llewellyn.com

KONSTANTINOS

Nocturnal

Witchcraft

MAGICK AFTER DARK

2002
Llewellyn Publications
St. Paul, Minnesota 55164-0383, U.S.A.

First Edition
First Printing, 2002

Author photo by David Armstrong
Book design by Donna Burch
Cover art and design by Kevin R. Brown
Editing by Karin Simoneau

Library of Congress Cataloging-in-Publication Data
Konstantinos, 1972–
    Nocturnal Witchcraft : magick after dark / Konstantinos.
        p.   cm.
    Includes bibliographical references and index.
    ISBN 0-7387-0166-1
        I. Magic. [I. Night—Miscellanea.] I. Title

    BF1611 .K655 2002
    133.4'3—dc21   2001050443

Llewellyn Worldwide does not participate in, endorse, or have any authority or responsibility concerning private business transactions between our authors and the public.
    All mail addressed to the author is forwarded but the publisher cannot, unless specifically instructed by the author, give out an address or phone number.
    Any Internet references contained in this work are current at publication time, but the publisher cannot guarantee that a specific location will continue to be maintained. Please refer to the publisher's website for links to authors' websites and other sources.

Llewellyn Publications
A Division of Llewellyn Worldwide, Ltd.
P.O. Box 64383, Dept. 0-7387-0166-1
St. Paul, MN 55164-0383, U.S.A.
www.llewellyn.com

♻ Printed in the United States of America on recycled paper

Other Books by Konstantinos

Vampires: The Occult Truth

Summoning Spirits: The Art of Magical Evocation

Contact the Other Side: 7 Methods for Afterlife Communication

Forthcoming Books by Konstantinos

Gothic Grimoire

Contents

Introduction

Are You One of Nightkind?

Do you dress in black? Favor silver jewelry? . . . Does being surrounded by the shadows, by the essence of night, appeal to you? Such dark tendencies may have manifested in you very early in life, affecting more than just the way you dress, the books you read, and the music you listen to.

Perhaps your nocturnal nature awakened in you a need for an alternative spirituality. At first this calling might have resulted in a desire to become aware of the unseen world. That urge likely evolved into a sense that there is something almost tangible in the night, calling you.

You are not alone.

If you've picked up this book, you may just be one of those souls who walk an often misunderstood spiritual path. You may be one of nightkind.

Traditional Wicca and other occult currents may have looked enticing at first, but could have left you feeling a bit alienated, as was the case with me. Most of these paths have evolved, through group input, to suit the greatest common denominator: to resonate with those who favor both solar and lunar energies.

Some of us live for the night, however. Some of us only feel a need for the light of the moon.

Yet where to look for mysteries related to our nature? Most occult books that approach the subject of darkness do so in a flawed way, assuming all their readers are seeking evil rites. If you're like me, however, you don't consider yourself evil, don't feel any attraction to the shallow philosophies of those who worship the devil. You know, inherently, that the concepts of dark and light have nothing to do with good and evil. As we'll see in chapter I, a soul is guided by an essence—in our case a nocturnal lure—that does not determine one's spiritual destiny, but the route taken to get there.

This book is for all who know that the nocturnal path is for them. I hope you'll find in the Craft of Night everything that you seek.

Of course, not everyone reading this book seeks to closely follow the currents described within. That's fine, too. We're all meant to resonate with varying shades of light and dark, to make the universe a diverse place. Perhaps you've sought out this alternative guide to Witchcraft because you wish to see if it contains any new rites or practices that you can incorporate into your own version of the Craft or other mystical path.

I promise you'll find such new experiences within.

Imagine divining with the night and reading minds, or enhancing your personal magnetism and affecting how others perceive you. How about taking spellcasting to a level you thought only possible in fantasy novels? You will learn how to alter reality, as well as master contacting aspects of the unseen world in ways you never thought possible.

The Gods and Goddesses of Night await you in the pages that follow, as do other universal energies, some as misunderstood as perhaps you've felt yourself to be.

Be you nightkind or curious seeker, welcome. We're about to explore nocturnal mysteries that have never before been gathered in one place.

Part One

The Craft of Nightkind

Chapter One

Embracing Darkness

Imagine an equal-armed cross—see it in the blank page to your left, stark black on a white background, like the ink on this page. Try it. See this icon of two intersecting poles.

Got it?

This is the simplest way to illustrate a principle that has confused humankind for ages. Through this icon we can understand the relationship of good and evil to the essences of light and dark.

Each of the poles in this simple cross represents a pair of misunderstood opposites. Just so we all see the diagram the same way, let's label it. We'll call the vertical pole good/evil, with good on top. The horizontal pair is light/dark, with light on the left. While these two pairs work together in a way we'll explore here, they are not the same.

The vertical pair represents our success or failure as human beings and immortal souls. We're all truly meant to accomplish good, and to become better individuals—to become, in essence, more like the Source that created us. This is the true purpose of most of the world's positive religions, including Wicca, where we perceive that the Source has both male and female aspects. We will explore later the concept of striving toward spiritual mastery, and introduce ways to access the energies of the Gods and Goddesses while we're still alive. For now, keep in mind that there is an ultimate reason for rising toward the good half of the pole on the vertical pair.

The horizontal pair determines the path we walk while advancing through a particular stage of our development. Not all of us are meant to surround ourselves with light and avoid the shadows. The ancients understood the concept of the nocturnal path well, which is why they identified and named more than just the light aspects of Divinity. As we'll get to in the next chapter, the various names given to Gods and Goddesses do not imply that there are thousands of such beings all struggling for power. Rather, they are each manifestations of a particular aspect, dark or light, of the primal energy from which we all came. We name these energies to better establish a link to the Source while we're still here. Some of us identify better with the dark ones among these deities.

Success or failure, and the path we walk to get there—keep these aspects of the cross icon in mind. Through an understanding of the symbol you'll master an occult truth. Don't take my word for it, however. See now how this truth applies to you.

The Four Soul-Types

If you focus for a moment on the white space surrounding our simple diagram, you'll see that it makes up four quadrants. It is in one of these four that a soul's particular lifetime can be mapped. Remember plotting geometric points on a graph in high school? There you would mark a point by noting its X and Y coordinates, or how far away from center, up or down, and left or right it was. In much the same way, we can identify a soul-type by how good or evil, dark or light it may be. The closer to the center one is in either axis, the more neutral he or she is with respect to that axis's pair of energies.

In other words, we come to see that there are four categories of individuals possible, and that people in each type can possess varying degrees of the category's essence. Starting in the upper left corner of the cross's white space and moving counterclockwise, the four soul-types are: good-light, evil-light, evil-dark, and good-dark. Some of us are more good or evil than others, some more drawn to darkness or light, but we still fall somewhere within one of the four soul-types. We'll touch briefly on the first three, then focus more intensely on the last one—the one whose energies we'll be working with in this book.

Good-light is the soul-type that most people are really referring to when they mention or think of the concept of good. People in this category include many (but not all) Wiccans and so-called New Agers. But one doesn't need to walk a spiritual path to be in this category. Anyone who is moral, loves brightness, and spreads joy honestly is good-light. These are also often the people who feel uplifted, for instance, by major-key music and inspirational fiction or feel-good tales. As an extreme example, some of the world's religion founders, such as Christ and Buddha, were of this soul-type. Whether the followers of such masters and the infrastructures of their and other organized religions live up to the good-light label, however, is open for debate. Speaking of living up to a path, were someone to fail at being good-light there is a decent chance they'd end up evil-light.

An overlooked type, evil-light is the sinister companion to good-light and the trickiest of the four groups to identify. Those of this soul-type seem at a glance to be moral individuals. Evil-light people may gather around them all the trappings of asceticism and harmony, or just what the masses perceive as being bright and positive. But behind the facade, the evil-light have given up trying to be better individuals. Consider a corrupt televangelist (feel free to do some digging into your memories or your library's newspaper archives if you feel this is only a stereotype). Evil-light televangelists would surround themselves with light themes and choir song, yet bilk their followers of millions, claiming that the gathered cash is going toward something other than a new Mercedes or Tudor mansion. Other evil-light can include righteous activists who let the end justify the means (for example, pro-lifers who bomb abortion clinics). Evil-light can even encompass corrupt executives who give to charity (as a good tax write-off) and frequent merry parties and even church, but who cheat in their business and personal dealings without regard for others.

Evil-dark, the true opposite of good-light, is the category that most people simplistically label as evil. Remember, the four categories can manifest in people in varying degrees. In the realm of the occult, evil-dark individuals can be the often harmless devil worshippers who value material goods and fun over their souls and the welfare of others, or can be the more sadistic individuals who perform black magic and human sacrifice. In the everyday world, common criminals often fit this category, although they can just as easily be evil-light.

Remember, the two evil soul-types are ones of failure. Whether a fallen one was good-light or good-dark before his or her sour turn determines, usually, whether he or she will become evil-light or evil-dark.

Unfortunately, most people are unaware of the nature of soul-types and mistake good-dark ones as being "bad." This is not surprising, considering that evil-dark people like devil worshippers get the most public attention, being ever vigilant for opportunities to spread their sinister propaganda. Conversely, the good-dark who succeed at the ultimate goal of adepthood or spiritual mastery do not attract as much attention, being mostly silent about their accomplishments.

Who are these good-dark? What makes someone a potential night-kind or Nocturnal Witch?

Allow me to violate traditional writing style here. Although I listed the four soul-types and explained three of them, we're going to pause for a moment before revealing the driving forces behind the good-dark. You'll see why as you read on.

Why We're Here

No one likes to be labeled. By no means am I introducing the concept of the four soul-types to pigeonhole people into stereotypes they have to follow. In fact, I resisted giving too many examples of the types of people who fall into the soul-type groups to prevent too much stereotyping. I'd rather each reader look around and identify the energies at work in the world, rather than immediately assume all is as it seems at a glance.

I'm relaying the information regarding soul-types as a gentle reminder that the dark and light energies represented in our cross icon are powerful, and that it's best to work with the energies present in your life. After all:

You chose to be the way you are.

You chose, before ever entering this world, what essences and correspondences, dark or light, to surround yourself with. And this is likely not the first time you made such a choice.

We're speaking of reincarnation, of course, and the active role we take in planning each of our returns.

The belief in reincarnation is so widespread among the world's religions, Wicca included, that people who *don't* believe in it are in the minority. And one of the biggest groups not to officially accept reincarnation—Christians—seems to contain more than a few who embrace the concept. As for how many Christians feel this way . . . well, that's beyond the scope of this work.

Most of you reading this are Witches, or would like to be, after all!

And maybe more than a few of you are nocturnal, like I am, but we'll return to that thread soon.

Why do so many people believe in reincarnation? Not because they're told to do so. How many people in this era believe in or stick to concepts simply because they're told "that's the way it is" by someone or some organization? The numbers are dwindling. We're more than ever in an age of free thought, which is why Witchcraft and other paths that let their practitioners take responsibility for their actions are becoming more accepted.

The real reason most people believe in reincarnation is simple: Reincarnation is the only concept that makes sense once you open yourself to the worlds of mysticism and free thought.

Remember, the point of all religion is to help us reunite with the Creator. This is taken an extra step in mystical paths like Wicca, which embrace magick (often spelled, as you may know, with a final "k" to differentiate it from stage magic). Magick is a tool, an applied science based on occult principles that we'll be exploring in great depth. The most important aspect of magick worth pointing out here, however, is that we can use it to help us perfect ourselves and become more attuned with Divine energies. Since, ultimately, we imperfect souls must strive to achieve adepthood, or spiritual mastery, magick can be seen as a way to reach this goal faster. But whether we use magick or not, we can't expect to become perfect over the course of even a record-setting 120-year lifespan.

Mastery takes lifetimes.

Think about it. If our highest goal is to reunite with the Source, we have to become more like the Source. I don't mean we have to be omniscient or omnipotent . . . just "omniexperienced." The Source is everything, as evidenced by the countless names that are tied to limitless attributes that have been given to the Gods and Goddesses throughout the ages. We, too, need to tap into everything, to challenge ourselves with whatever the universe offers. And we have to open ourselves to as many of these experiences as possible, while deriving from them every lesson we can. It wouldn't do to try and be a doctor, lawyer, missionary, and mechanic in one life, for instance. You wouldn't be able to get much from any of these professions, as you'd spend most of your time trying to become each. We are meant to fully experience certain aspects of life each time we return.

Each life or incarnation is a set period of training. Before we come here, to earth, our souls decide which lessons and experiences we need to have to advance one more sphere toward the realm of perfection. We'll deal more with the mechanics of the afterlife in chapter 13, where we'll meet the personified essences of dying and rebirth—Death with a capital *D*, if you will. For now, let's simply work on the assumption that each life is filled with purpose. You'll realize that this assumption is a fact later on, through firsthand experience.

This is a good time to point out that I'll never ask you to take my word for anything I write in this book (or in any other). Nocturnal Witchcraft must be experienced. The concepts and techniques in these pages are real and awaiting your personal interaction with them. I'm ready to let you prove to yourself that what I say is true.

Now, back to your choices in each life. If you're familiar with reincarnation, you may have heard that we choose all aspects of our new life: who our parents will be, what kind of physical body we'll inhabit (including its gender), and the types of major challenges we will encounter. As far as I can tell from my sources, many of which will become clear to you later on, this is indeed how reincarnation works. But none of these choices we make account for how we'll work with the challenges and experiences awaiting us here on earth. Consider how different you may feel from even others you've met who are involved in the occult. Are you drawn to quite the same books, the same practices?

The unique journey that awaits us in each life depends on which current we'll most closely align ourselves with.

The world is full of brightness and shadow, and energies that sympathetically vibrate with these polarities. By working with dark or light currents in each life we are ensuring we can have the most complete range of experiences while on earth. Some may argue that it's important to work with both dark and light in a lifetime. This may be true for some, but those who feel this way are most likely souls who have been here so many times that they're ready to balance out a few dark and light points before achieving adepthood.

I think most of us have a few lifetimes left, however. Don't you feel the same way? And even if we are on our last incarnation, our souls do not lie to us. If you're drawn to this book's mysteries, there's a very good chance you've selected the dark path, for at least this part of your life. For me, the dark path has lasted since I can remember, making it decades long. It has lead to more than a bit of confusion, which I'll share in these pages, but also lead me to a simple understanding:

It's perfectly acceptable to stick with a current for either a lifetime or just part of it.

Again, your soul knows what it's here to accomplish. As long as the night calls you, answer. As long as shadows envelop your positive work, learn to influence these forces to accomplish amazing things.

Just as people change religions, they can change the polarity of their soul-type. Sometimes this is unfortunate, as we hinted at, because it could mean someone is going from one of the good types to the evil side. It's also possible, however, to go from dark to light, or vice versa, and remain good. Not all good-dark will remain so—for instance, they may switch to good-light. But I still suspect it's much easier to change the names of the Gods you pray to than to change what clicks for you on a deep level. God and Goddess names, as we'll see, are only sonic keys that open doorways to Divine energy. Dark and light energies are the hallways containing these doorways.

A Personal Take on a Soul-Type

Now, who are the good-dark?

You likely already know the answer. If it's your soul-type in this life, you could explain it to me using the specifics that apply to you. And if you don't feel it's your soul-type, good-dark's energies (at least the ones I've hinted at so far) would seem different than the ones you feel, and you'd be able to explain the soul-type by way of contrast.

Either way, you know what good-dark means through personal experience. I'll just add some of my ideas to the mix here, also by calling on experience.

Of all my books, this is the one in which I feel I can most deeply connect with the psyche of its readers. While my other books have dealt with specific occult phenomena or practices, this is the first one to deal with my personal path.

Here goes . . . it's sharing time.

As a child, I would read tales of Greek mythology and believe that the Gods and Goddesses were real. This more than "freaked out" my Greek Orthodox parents, no doubt, who had to field questions about how Zeus and Aphrodite related to the God they were worshiping every Sunday. While they played along with my interest in mythology for a while, they soon began subtly avoiding conversations about what the ancients believed resided at the top of Mount Olympus. Christian parents can't find it too comforting when their young son is praying to pagan Gods—or when he becomes older and does the same thing, for that matter.

Finding Zeus and his pantheon was easy. Although I was born in the United States, all of my family came from Greece. Some were still there when I was a child, and as a result I maintained a link with the country's mysteries through these relatives. Most relevant here was the access I had to richly illustrated books that my dad's mother would bring when she visited. In these pages I met, in vivid tales and colorful artwork, the Gods of old, all before I was old enough to go to the library by myself.

Soon after, I discovered through my own probing of mythologies that other cultures had similar Gods and Goddesses. It began to make sense that the world had been worshiping the same Divine energies for millennia, only using different names for them. The pantheons of Mesopotamia and the region's dark magickal systems particularly interested me. While I could have argued that through a study of the

Greek Gods I was connecting to a part of my heritage, I couldn't explain my interest in other Gods and Goddesses, first the Sumerian deities and later even the Egyptian ones.

This deep interest in mythology led me to an early belief in reincarnation, before I even heard the word. I began to feel that if it was only the ancients who believed in these Gods I was "discovering," then it was possible that I might have been among these ancients at one time. I felt that I might have loved the old Gods and Goddesses in other lives.

All this eventually resulted in a courtship with formal Wicca that began in the late 1980s. When I first encountered the religion, it appeared ideal for me. I had already found myself intensely drawn to magick and the occult, and resented the claims of organized religion that such mysticism was evil. In Wicca I found a religion that not only embraced magick, but which also was based on the belief that the Gods and Goddesses were real.

It all seemed almost perfect for me, and I trusted that the things that didn't feel quite right would work themselves out in time. So I began practicing the Craft, giving it my all for a while.

After a few years of involvement, I wrote my first book proposal . . . the subject was the Sumerian Goddess Inanna. The project was one my soon-to-be publisher wanted me to pursue, and I began it. However, as my long-time readers know, this book was never released. Why? Because I never completed it.

Around this time in the early 1990s, I began finding it difficult to balance my dark interests with the brightness inherent in most iterations of modern paganism. In hindsight, I realize that writing that Inanna book might have helped me immensely—I needed to go through my own descent into the Underworld, like this Goddess, and emerge changed (more on such a descent later).

Instead, I turned away and tried to explore where I fit into the religious half of my mystical path. I already knew what I wanted from the magickal half—I wanted to approach adepthood. Yet such a goal is not in itself a religion. Religion is that part of your path that helps you keep in touch with Divinity while you're trying to ultimately reunite with it.

The books I've written are therefore accessible to those of all religions. I knew when writing them that the choice of that part of someone's path—religion—is always very personal, relating more to one's life purpose than to the decisions of, say, his or her parents. I stuck to the simple guideline that my readers should find ways of connecting to the Source for themselves, just like I needed a way to connect with Divinity that didn't seem alien because of my nature.

My nature. What was "wrong" with me? Why could I never connect with the light themes I kept encountering in religion?

How I wish someone had been there to tell me:

When the essence of the shadows and darkness empowers you, yet you don't feel evil, you are good-dark.

I can think of no better definition. Dark allure is not something you grow out of when it's really a part of your "calling" or life purpose. Even after decades, I'm no less drawn to the night energies described in the chapters that follow.

How I also wish that someone pointed out to me that good-dark types can use their nature to better connect to the Source, as well as to the unseen world. The path of night can very much be one of enlightenment. After I realized what my path was—a process I'll discuss in chapter 3—I strengthened and reaffirmed my connection with Witchcraft. Once again, the knowledge of and communion with both God and Goddess aspects of Divinity became my religion. The right aspects of Divinity for me, that is.

In this book you'll learn how you can make the Craft work for you if you're good-dark. Of course, you're free to choose whichever religion is right for you—Witchcraft is not the only path out there.

Just make sure that the religious path you choose works with your soul-type, not against it. You'll save yourself much grief by doing so.

Having identified the types of callings that good-dark feel, I'll refrain from giving too many examples of who these people may be. We are an elusive lot!

You'll find good-dark in both mystical and more material roles. The former type we'll explore in this book, the latter you see everyday. Good-dark are more than just those who frequent dark nightclubs and never harm anyone—nightkind can take many forms.

Sometimes a good-dark person will feel the need to reflect his or her nature in choice of profession: A detective who works by night, chasing down crime while surrounded by settings that most find morbid, is likely good-dark; as is an artist who feels great joy in sharing his or her dark work with the world. And, possibly the most relevant example:

Good-dark may be someone like you.

Maybe I can spare you some of the searching I went through. In chapter 3, we'll take a brief look at how I found the Gods and Goddesses of Night, and delve into how you may contact them yourself. Let's continue now with a look at how nightkind's nature meshes with the tenets of Witchcraft.

Witchy Ethics

Witchcraft can help you keep the "good" in your good-dark path. Despite the slanderous lies said about its pagan roots during the Inquisition, and said about it still by those mentally living in the past, Witchcraft or Wicca is a religion and way of life that is surrounded by only positive energies and ethics.

This book is not intended to be a primer on traditional Wicca—we'll be examining the Craft from the perspective of nightkind. If this is the first book you're reading on Witchcraft, you may want to soon after supplement your reading with some of the new classics of modern paganism, listed here alphabetically by author: *The Complete Book of Witchcraft*, by Raymond Buckland, *Power of the Witch*, by Laurie Cabot, *Wicca: A Guide for the Solitary Practitioner*, by Scott Cunningham, and *To Ride a Silver Broomstick,* by Silver RavenWolf (see Suggested Reading for more information on all of these books).

We'll still go over some of the basics in this book, and all the chapters in part one contribute to this groundwork. Also, although what I'll be revealing in parts two and three is a bit more advanced and different than what you may encounter in other forms of Wicca, it still works perfectly in league with traditional Craft currents and positive ethics. Witchcraft has always been practiced in different ways by those with different interests. This is the primary reason there are so many traditions, ranging from Alexandrian to Celtic to Dianic, and on. Nocturnal Witchcraft can be thought of as the tradition that was always there, just never organized. It's the tradition that naturally suits the spiritual and physical needs of many nightkind.

With that said . . .

. . . what exactly is *good,* as far as Witches are concerned?

At the heart of the Wiccan way is the basic rede you've likely encountered before:

"An it harm none, do what ye will."

This goes for both magickal endeavors and mundane or purely physical workings. So what happens should you violate this rule? What are the penalties for either casting a spell against someone or swinging a fist at him or her?

Here's where the universal law of karma steps in. Karma is like a cosmic bank account of spiritual credits. Perform good deeds, and you build up positive credits with interest. Do evil against others or yourself, and you make a painful withdrawal of credits . . . with penalties.

Ever hear of the Law of Three? It states that whatever you do or send out will return to you threefold. I'm not sure if this could ever be quantified, but the general idea is that if you do a certain amount of good or evil in the world, even more good or evil will return to you. Personal experience has shown that this is the case, even if I can't vouch for an exactly threefold effect. Doing positive magick for others, for instance, has always resulted in more than just good feelings turning up in my life. And while I've never sent a "demon" after anyone, during the times in my life when I've succumbed to less than positive ways of acting I have felt the consequences.

We're not perfect . . . yet. Witchcraft and a healthy respect for karma can help us get there, however.

Karma's effects do not end with a particular lifetime, either. We sometimes carry either an abundance of blessings or a spiritual burden with us into future lives. More on this in chapter 13, however, when we discuss the afterlife.

Because of karma and our accountability for all our actions, walking one of the two evil paths described earlier always leads to ruin—in this life or the next. So, be you dark or light, do try to stay to the top or good side of our cross icon.

Temptation for things that are harmful for us or for others can begin to lead us astray from time to time. Expect temptation, in fact. How else could the universe teach us the lessons we're sent here to learn? For example, if your purpose in this life is to have a fulfilling relationship, perhaps because you betrayed someone in a past life, you would likely now face a temptation for infidelity that's much stronger than the one that led you astray when you lived in another time.

Perhaps it would be three times stronger?

Walking a positive path like the one described in this book can help immensely in your pursuit of adepthood. While this is certainly not the only book that deals with how to attain some mastery over oneself and occult forces, it is the only one that, again, focuses on how to do so in the shadows.

The Most Important Embrace

Before we move on from this chapter and its theme of how the forces of good and dark can be intertwined, we need to experience one last truth, reveal one last secret:

Like attracts like in the unseen world.

Just as doing good karmically attracts good, working with something representative of an energy attracts or influences that energy. This is the reason that voodoo dolls work, for example. By taking some personal items or body parts (nail clippings, a lock of hair) you can create a representation of someone and then act magickally, for good or evil, on this sympathetic representation.

Some forms of Witchcraft-based magick, such as candleburning or herbalism, are heavily based on sympathetic principles, using multiple associations such as colors or planetary influence to accomplish their tasks. Some of these rituals even take "like attracts like" a step further, being based around days or hours of the day that correspond to particular planetary energies. This is fine for such rites, and very effective.

We won't be concerning ourselves with this type of multi-correspondence magick here, however—our candles and incenses will all share a common attribute. For more on traditional candleburning and herbalism you'd do well to check out books by Raymond Buckland and Scott Cunningham, respectively. Another major type of sympathetic correspondence in magick is when rites are designed around the four magickal elements of earth, air, fire, and water. Our work with these elements will for the most part be limited to their influence on a magickal circle.

In this book, our primary focus will be on establishing sympathetic links with two other major forces in the universe: darkness and lunar energy.

Nocturnal Witches can use all forms of magick, of course, and I urge you to explore all manner of occult techniques. They will work perfectly in the circles you'll learn to cast here. But to succeed with the advanced techniques in this book you won't need to worry about what day of the week to perform a rite or which assortment of colors to use in a working. You'll only have to follow the phase of the moon (for some rituals), and as for color . . .

. . . black and silver will work for most everything.

Black is the absence of color and draws into itself all colors and energies from the universe, including the power associated with the decreasing and New or Dark Moon. Silver (or white, in a pinch) can also be used for certain nocturnal workings where you wish to call up lunar currents during an increasing or Full Moon.

But following lunar phases is still not required for all the workings in this book; rather, the phase of the moon is just helpful to certain workings. Nocturnal Witches can derive the greatest power from tapping into one primary sympathetic link—the link that best represents the essence they chose to align themselves with in this life.

We get power from the night, of course.

Everything in this book will work better after the sun has set, regardless of the phase of the moon. You can make these rites work by day, but like any other magickal working, a nocturnal ritual should be surrounded by sympathetic energies to ensure the most potent results. For a Nocturnal Witch this is simply a matter of waiting until night.

The daytime world is, for most people, the time when mundane (but often necessary) tasks are performed. We usually work in these hours, forcing our brains to stick to a type of activity that is not conducive to magick. When the sun is high and the masses are about, we all interact with the physical plane to a greater degree, shutting down access to our subtler senses and powers.

Later we'll see how to awaken these hidden faculties while most others prepare to sleep or after they've drifted off.

Although you won't have to radically change which hours you spend awake, some of you will have to shift them slightly to get maximum benefit from the techniques taught in this book. I say some of you, because chances are a good many of you already try to get some enjoyment from the dark hours—they likely have voiced their call to you before.

Books on traditional Wicca often urge readers to spend more time in nature. This is fine, when you're planning on working with natural magick or herbalism, for instance.

I have a simpler request to make of you. If you wish to spend more time by sea or forest brook, or appreciating the wind or the cool soil beneath you, be sure to try and do so when the only light around is that of the stars and moon. You'll then be experiencing nocturnal nature, which may be your nature.

And the powers described herein will come.

Chapter Two

Wicca by Night

To live as a Witch, you need not follow a strict routine. There's no building to report to weekly, no alleged spiritual rulers to obey.

However, there are some Craft traditions that can enrich your life if you choose to follow them.

We have many days—okay, nights in our case—that can be celebrated for the energies they lend to our lives. In all, we recognize eight sabbats or holidays, thirteen Full Moons, and thirteen Dark Moons to choose from.

Available to us is the use of wonderful tools, ranging from simple to elaborate, that can help us succeed at magickal and religious rites. We use these in conjunction with personal altars to form the center of our own sacred spaces. We can be with the Gods anywhere we choose.

As for the specific ways we celebrate our religion, and the specific implements we use to do so, all these vary. Except for those who work in established traditions, most Witches are comfortable with picking and choosing what works best for them in experiencing the Old Religion.

In this book and in the companion book, *Gothic Grimoire*, we'll be exploring a specific set of practices that can reasonably be called a tradition. However, the Nocturnal Tradition, which we won't spend much time labeling as such in this book, is not meant to be a rigid structure. Use as many of its dark aspects in your own path as you feel comfortable with. Feel free to modify these nighttime practices; the never-before-published basics taught in this book can be used to train for and enhance most any type of magick. The companion volume's rites, also being released for the first time, can help you embrace Nocturnal Witchcraft more fully.

In this chapter we will introduce some of the traditional nights of the year and the tools used for celebrating them, as well as many other rites. If you're an established Witch, by the time you finish reading this overview you may have a better idea of which aspects of this dark system will mesh well with your work. Readers new to the Craft will learn more about the dark take on Wicca covered in our system.

Nights of Power

In books about a particular ethnic type of paganism or about a certain Wiccan tradition, a section like this one would typically contain a cycle of myths describing the eight days or nights of power. We'd then follow the stories of specific Gods and Goddesses, as reflected by the changing seasons. Such a look at the Wheel of the Year, as the group of holidays is called, is certainly valid. The eight holidays do form a cycle that can be applied to the legend of, say, a particular dying God. However, in this book we'll avoid repeatedly focusing on any one pantheon when describing the Wheel, touching only briefly on the most universal associations of the Gods to the eight nights, including a few names where most relevant.

What you'll be reading here is my explanation of the major energies present in each of the eight nights of power or sabbats. Do not acknowledge these eves out of fear—you won't be breaking some commandment by ignoring them. Celebrate the sabbats to tap the natural energies that cycle through our bodies, and to better connect to various aspects of Divinity throughout the year. But don't wait for a sabbat to act on some magickal need. For most purposes, the nights of the Full and Dark Moons can be more practically applied to the challenges that regularly arise in life. Waiting until Halloween to do a divination rite, for example, isn't always practical.

As for exactly how to celebrate the sabbats, we won't have room to cover that. As mentioned, this book is in many ways an introduction to a system. Using the basics you learn in its three parts, you may create your own rituals to flesh out what Nocturnal Witchcraft means to you, including the way you wish to honor the sabbats.

Note that although the holidays are ancient, many have undergone transmutation by the Church. Such adaptation of traditions is common when one religion tries to convert followers of another. We'll be pointing out these parallels, even when they're obvious, to better clarify the core energies at work during any particular sabbat.

Samhain, or *Halloween* (October 31), can be thought of as the night when the pagan year ends and begins anew. An end of the harvest, this night marks death and the promise of rebirth. Just as the crops will return and the year's cycle of seasons will return . . . so shall those of us who pass on. While the word Samhain is Celtic, the celebration of death and rebirth on this night has been attributed to various cultures across continents. They all sensed that as the earth stands balanced between death and life, so do all who attune to this night's energies, which is why I prefer to use the more-recognized name Halloween for this universal night. It is the time when the veil between the worlds is at its sheerest, and when we can most easily peer through—a great night for divination and necromancy, as well as for celebrating the dark months that are approaching. Like many of the pagan holidays, Halloween was Christianized by the Church, this time as a hallowed eve before All Saints and All Souls. We celebrate the night in religious ways, too, commemorating the idea of the dying God, who ultimately symbolizes the cycle of death and rebirth.

On the Winter Solstice, or *Yule* (around December 20), we celebrate the start of the new solar year or the coming of new light. Odd for a Nocturnal Witch to celebrate this? Not at all, when you consider that our planet's year is charted by how it moves around the sun. Interestingly enough, this celebration is held on the longest night of the year, making this quite a powerful time for we nocturnal folk, too! In addition to providing more dark hours to sympathetically link to, Yule is an excellent time to renew our personal goals and attempt life-changing magic—to be reborn, so to speak. Traditionally, the birth of the God to the Mother Goddess is celebrated at this time. Festivities for this birth would in some cultures last for days; the peak of this celebration in Rome, around December 25, was once called *sol invictus*, or the feast of the unconquered sun, whose light would be returning increasingly to each day. To give its new followers something to do during the height of Yule festivities, the Church chose this time to be the celebration of Christmas. Quite a stretch, considering that archaeologists believe Christ was likely born in March. Still, having the celebrations at the same time has led to the modernization of some interesting pagan customs. Ask any who do so why they decorate a tree or hang lights and mistletoe at this time. They might not be aware that they're really embracing Druidic and other pagan ways of commemorating Yule.

Candlemas (February 2), also called Imbolc, has evolved into a national holiday where we all await a furry critter's weather prediction. Yet impressed as we all are by the groundhog's 50 percent accuracy— unbelievably, spring will really be six weeks later, regardless of the critter's shadow—the reason this day was selected for recognition still holds power. Halfway through winter, Candlemas reminds us that it won't always be this cold. Something new is beginning—the tide is turning from increasing cold to gradual warming. A fire is on the horizon for the coming days, and Goddesses like Brigid were honored to reflect this. Because it is a night of future promise, it is an amazing time to begin something new. Incidentally, Candlemas is the name that evolved when Imbolc was Christianized into a day honoring Saint

Brigit rather than Goddess Brigid (we won't get into the tales told to explain her as a missionary rather than a deity). So why are we using the name Candlemas here? It's got a nice ring to it for those of us who work by candlelight, wouldn't you say? And you'll need much candle-light, as the dark hours are still blessedly long at Candlemas.

But the night's dominance recedes, leading to the Spring Equinox, or *Ostara* (around March 21), when manifestations of dark and light are equal. This is our last chance to appreciate at least twelve hours of night. Although it recognizes the return of the sun, this holiday is not only a solar one. Some of you may recall that I only mentioned a dying God when discussing Halloween. The dying Goddesses who descended into the Underworld, such as Inanna and Demeter, are best recognized on this night when the earth returns from its infertile slumber. A per-fect time for any magick related to fertility of any kind, from repro-ductive matters to, say, a growing career. In fact, the first Full Moon after Spring Equinox will only heighten such powers. The name Ostara actually comes from a lunar Goddess, Eostara, who is also best wor-shipped on the first Full Moon after the Equinox. You can therefore think of this holiday's energies as ranging over a period of as many as twenty-seven nights, except on those occasional years when the holiday lands on a Full Moon. Guess what holiday the Church decided to cel-ebrate on the Sunday following Eostara's Equinox Full Moon?

Called May Day, *Beltane* (after sunset April 30 into May 1) is an-other feast of fertility, marking the start of the second half of the year (recall that Halloween began the year). Traditionally this was a night of bonfires, followed by a day of rites such as the weaving of the May-pole. By this time in the year, we have fully assimilated nature's spring energies, and so has the Goddess, who is now pregnant with the God. This is an excellent time for sex magick or other rites of culmination, including follow-ups to magick that was begun on Ostara.

Midsummer's Eve (around June 21) is actually the first night of sum-mer, and is the other Solstice. Because it is the shortest night of the year, it is the best night for nightkind to remain awake until sunrise, thereby recharging our nocturnal energies and avoiding walking around too much during the day hours. The Sun God is at his highest power now, after all, and those with the strongest affinity for night may feel uncomfortable, and may even find themselves temporarily out of touch with their newly developed abilities (like those revealed in parts two and three). As on Halloween, the veil between the worlds is believed to be thin at this time. Many customs call for somehow spotting unseen etheric creatures or the invisible world itself on this night. These associations likely came about from the fact that with so little nighttime, our dreams and reality may merge from sleep deprivation. No point going against such built-up thoughts or thoughtforms—stay awake and see what happens! See what gathers around the perimeter of your magick circle.

By *Lammas*, or Lughnassad (August 2), we begin a harvesting period in the year. As few of us are likely farmers in this century, Lammas is the time we begin to reap what we've figuratively sown all year. This is an excellent time for prosperity rituals, and to perhaps begin looking for a new job. The nights are just beginning to get noticeably longer, and we can feel the promise of what for many nightkind is the most cherished season: fall. The harvesting energies that awaken on this night lead us into Mabon.

Mabon, or the Fall Equinox (around September 21), is when night and day are once again equal, yet this time with the coming of dominating darkness. The Sun God is about to be vanquished and recede until his own descent on Halloween—of course, the Goddess is readying to have him be reborn on Yule. The peak harvest, this is when you can culminate prosperity rites. Also, it's a great time to begin fall revelry, including preparing for Halloween. Know that nocturnal powers will have increased intensity for the next six months. Begin thinking along the lines of accessing the unseen.

From Dark to Full

While the eight sabbats celebrate and help us tap into diverse natural energies over the course of the year, the cycles of the moon allow us to access certain powers on a more regular basis. A particular half of the cycle, when the moon is either increasing or decreasing, is never more than thirteen nights away—a particular absolute phase, such as Full or Dark, is at most twenty-seven nights away. For nightkind, the cycle of the moon can be thought of as a more practical and powerful one to work with in ritual than is the Wheel of the Year. In most cases, you'll want to save the sabbats for really special workings, and rely on the moon and nighttime in general to deal with whatever magickal needs arise in your life on a regular basis.

Considered to begin on the night of the New or Dark Moon, the cycle of the moon's phases is approximately twenty-eight days long (it's really just a few hours longer than twenty-seven days, but it only makes sense to round up when you're dealing with what is the beginning of the next "day" in a month).

The Dark Moon is when no silver light shines upon us and we discern only a circular shade of black creeping through the velvet night sky. In this time of starlight alone, dark powers are at their greatest. Think of the Dark Moon as the time when night's energies work in their purest form, as the time when your own connection to your nature can work its magick for you. On this night you would best be able to accomplish any of the purely mental techniques taught in part two. It is also the best night to celebrate a connection to the Gods and Goddesses associated with either the Dark Moon or Night Personified.

Over the next thirteen nights or so the moon is increasing. You can work with this growing lunar influence by performing magick for some type of growing or increase, too. This includes rites for fertility, money, better careers or homes, and even boosts to health.

The next night of power is the Full Moon, when lunar influences are at their peak. While not opposite in nature to the pure nocturnal magick best performed on the Dark Moon, Full Moon magick is when multinight prosperity rites can peak, or when a single, powerful effect can be tried for. Celebrating the Full Moon also is a terrific way to achieve better attunement with the lunar Gods and Goddesses.

The final thirteen nights or so of the cycle are when the moon is decreasing, once again approaching the powers of pure night. Magick for banishings of all kinds will work best during this decreasing period; this includes exorcising evil or dangerous influences from life. You can set up rituals for protection, or for getting rid of bad habits that can be destructive—the idea of banishing can be very loosely interpreted.

Note that in all these examples, we are not really referring to the chunk of rock that floats in the sky. Rather, we're dealing with the sympathetic link to an aspect of nature that the moon represents. Just as night is the greatest link we have to darkness, the moon is the one object that works with the dark hours and cycles through them as we do. Through its increasing and decreasing intensity of reflected light, it sympathetically simulates our ability to work with varying amounts of darkness. While following its cycles is not necessary, doing so can help a nightkind person's connection to dark energies. The lunar currents are real—powerful enough even to affect a woman's monthly cycle if she lives outdoors or somehow closer to the moon's influence. Use the powerful influence of the moon when you can.

Following the cycles of the moon can also be a potent aid to magickal training. In chapter 4 you'll learn a simple dedication rite that will help you align with nocturnal currents over the time leading to your self-initiation. A full self-initiation rite is included in the *Gothic Grimoire*, as you really shouldn't perform such a rite until after you've begun applying the techniques revealed here in this book. After your dedication and before your initiation, you'll want to practice basic circle casting on a regular basis. You will also want to begin to know night's deities.

One of the best ways to regularly practice circle casting and deity attunement is by celebrating both Full and Dark Moons for a few months. In addition to providing extra reasons to create sacred space and invoke the Gods and Goddesses, moon rites help you become accustomed to the cycles we're talking about. Feeling the cycles at work around you will change how you perceive night; becoming accustomed to lunar energies will also make you far more psychically sensitive to all manner of unseen currents around you.

So do consider celebrating as many Full and Dark Moon circles as you can. Both these, and general circle casting, are covered in chapter 4.

Setting Up a Nocturnal Altar

Prepare to be shocked, especially if you've done more than some dabbling in ceremonial magick. Nocturnal Witchcraft does not require many tools—the few you'll need to get started can be acquired in an afternoon. Further, as you progress in your practice, you'll see that many nocturnal rites can be performed with nothing but your own growing, internal power. One of the beautiful aspects of this system or tradition is that it relies heavily on your awareness of your own nature for success.

Ritual is psychodrama. For the most part, tools or ritual aids are only there to help us jar our subconscious minds into an altered state. Think of our waking consciousness as being a barrier to psychic and magickal abilities. Conditioned to dealing with purely physical aspects of the world, our waking minds block out the subtle states we seek in magickal rites. That's why ritual is so important. Its actions and accoutrements help us break down our barriers and be more receptive to the unseen energies and world around us.

In the beginning of your practice, you'll want to use whatever physical tools you can. Eventually, however, you'll find that more and more magickal workings are possible by simply employing your will, preferably under the cover of shadow.

To reflect the recurring power of darkness, some of the nocturnal tools are reused rite to rite, night to night. However, to reflect the individual power each night has over the four magickal elements of the universe, you will also use some temporary tools in each working— that is, some of your tools will be used only a few times then discarded (don't panic about cost—you'll see in a moment how logical this discarding is for certain items).

First you'll need an altar—a place to rest all your tools during a working. It should be a table or some kind of similar construct that is about as tall as your waist when you're standing. This place will be your nocturnal altar. If you have a table that can be set aside for this purpose, terrific. If not, you can use one that has a "mundane" role, too—each time you cast a magick circle the table will automatically be purified. You'll also need a black altar cloth to cover the table; this should not be reused as something else, however. Only spread this cloth over your altar when you are preparing to lay out your tools for a ritual.

Now, on to those tools, beginning with the few you'll use repeatedly to invoke darkness. In chapter 4 you'll see how to dedicate these permanent tools to your use in Nocturnal Witchcraft.

An active aid to magick is the athame, or black-handled knife of traditional Wicca. In our practice it would seem a no-brainer that its handle be black, but in actuality the reason for the color choice is based on the athame's use. As we said, black is the color that draws everything into itself. The athame is used to direct energy out of our bodies and toward some purpose. Therefore, having a black handle helps the athame draw energy from your projecting hand (the hand you write with) and channel this power out through the double-edged blade. These considerations—handle color and blade type—are not the only ones to keep in mind when shopping. Make sure the knife is comfortable to hold and feels almost natural in your hand. Its purpose is to be an extension of yourself, kind of like an extended finger or two; and in a pinch you can also use your pointer and middle fingers together for an athame. You'll use your athame predominantly for casting circles or charging objects with energy. Again, you'll most often hold the athame in your writing or projecting hand; however, there are certain ritual steps that call for a banishing or disruptive stroke to be made with the athame, in which case you'll hold it in the opposite or receiving hand.

More passive but equally powerful is what you can think of as a nocturnal portal. This is some type of round skrying tool that is black. You can choose to use a magick mirror—basically a piece of round glass with one side painted flat black (you look through the side of the glass disc that's unpainted). You can either make such a mirror yourself or buy one from a New Age store. A piece of round, flat obsidian works well, too. Or if you prefer, some kind of black crystal ball will make a fine portal. While this object's primary use is for skrying, the nocturnal portal should be on your altar for all rites, to help you connect with nocturnal energies and the hidden potential of the Dark Moon. How can a skrying tool accomplish this? The answer will become clear to you in part two.

On each side of your nocturnal portal should be placed a black taper candle—you can use silver for a Full Moon celebration. You choose the style of holder, preferably black, as these will always be on your altar, but the candle must be a taper. Votives that burn inside glass can cause refractions of light that will adversely affect those times when you do wish to skry. The tapers will have to be placed just far enough back on either side of the portal so that they do not show up as reflections inside the portal. But we'll get to that when we describe how to tilt or orient your skrying device for use.

Well in front of your properly oriented portal you should place a censer so that it is not seen in the reflection of the angled skrying device. The censer can be a simple holder for stick or cone incense, or an elaborate ceramic bowl for burning coals on which you'll sprinkle powder incense. It's your choice, just make sure it's black. The only permanent altar tools that don't need to be black are your representations of the God and Goddess.

Farther behind and to the sides of the tapers, place your God and Goddess images or symbols. These can change, depending on your working. For instance, if you're working with a particular deity, you might try to get a statue or picture of him or her. Or you can use symbols related to the deity. Deciding which representations to put at these two far corners (God to the right, Goddess to the left) is up to you. While you will add things, symbols, to your altar for invocations of

certain deities, you should always have some representation of each polarity present.

The last permanent item you'll need is one that goes on you, not
on your altar. Regardless of whether you wear black all the time, you
will need a special black outfit saved only for ritual. A robe is ideal, as
it helps you immediately establish in your mind that you are about to
do something out of the ordinary. However, some people feel uncomfortable or even pretentious in a robe. For such folks, a robe wouldn't
do at all, causing only distractions during ritual. Make sure that the
garment you choose is a comfortable one, and special in that it is set
aside for serious ritual workings only—a casual dress, a cotton shirt
and pants, whatever, as long as it's black and used only for entering a
magickal state of mind.

Now we come to the temporary tools—the ones related to the
magickal elements. Recall, we said we'd only be working with the magickal elements when casting circles; this book's techniques only rely on
the elements being invited to share their energies to the perimeter of
sacred space. Elemental energies form a balanced field to surround
your place of working. The altar, however, should not contain a built-
up reserve of elemental energies; it should remain a nocturnal focus
point. In our dark tradition, therefore, elemental tools that rest on the
altar should only be ones that serve a purpose for one or a few circle
castings, and which are then discarded.

For calling air you will use a stick of incense. This does not have to
be the scent you will keep burning in the censer for the remainder of
the rite you're performing, although it can be (if you're using a scent
just for calling air, try sandalwood or lavender). As you'll see in the circle casting described in chapter 4, what you do with this incense after
invoking the elements is up to you. However, during the air invocation,
the incense must be carried around without a censer, hence, it must be
a stick. Place this to the east edge of your altar before beginning a rite.

Fire will be called by a red candle, either votive or taper. Note that
you will only be using this for a few minutes, so even a birthday cake

candle would do! There's no need to have a candleholder handy, as the candle will not need to remain lit on the altar after you lift and light it for use during the circle casting. Keep the candle to the south on your altar.

For water you can use any cup filled with . . . you guessed it. The cup can even be paper, as you don't need to reuse it in ritual. However, depending on your environmental awareness, you might want to avoid plastic or Styrofoam (just a suggestion). Place the half-filled cup to the west on your altar.

Earth can be best represented by a small bit of salt. Some like to argue for the use of sea salt, claiming it is purer, and they're right in that respect. But when you consider the element that true sea salt has been associated with for all its prepowder-form existence, you'll find that ordinary supermarket salt is fine for an earth representation. Place three or four pinches of salt on a little bit of brown paper, such as a two-inch square of a shopping bag, or on a green or brown ceramic dish. Put this to the north on your altar.

Note that there is no need for a pentacle on the altar. Not because this is an unimportant symbol—it is. There's even a very special one on the cover of this book. The pentacle is the representation of spirit (the top point) coming above the four magickal elements in importance. Inverting the pentacle to two points up, as devil worshippers do, actually lowers your ability to impact the spirit world. Like many other Witches, I try to wear a one-point-up pentacle whenever possible (although I wear ankhs, too, for a reason I'll explain in chapter 13). It reminds us of our spiritual aims in life and beyond, and even brings some protection to the wearer by naturally repelling forces that do not adhere to such positive aims. Like attracts like, and opposites repel in the occult, after all.

But while the pentacle is an important symbol that we'll be using in our magick, a physical representation of it as a pentacle on the altar is not necessary. Rather, you will be creating an etheric one over your nocturnal portal with each circle casting. This will be the pentacle of spirit, and will tie you to the unseen world for the time you spend in the magick circle. As you'll find, it's not just pretty art, the pentacle on the cover of this book. You'll find that this is a loose artistic representation of an actual etheric form you'll create in ritual.

And now, on to the most powerful force that will be present in your dark circles and rites.

Chapter Three

Reaching the Dark Divine

The Source.

I like that word for Divinity. It reminds us that we came from somewhere, and that we have someplace to ultimately return.

Yet I could never pray directly to the Source, or hope to connect with it easily, by thinking of it in such a nameless, faceless form. As mentioned in chapter I, God and Goddess names provide us with a way to access Divine energy.

In this chapter I'll show you how to reach that energy.

Finding the Source

Imagine for a moment that the Source is just like a water source in a mountain. Whether it's a melting glacier or natural font, such a water source would reveal itself to those living in a forest surrounding the mountain, manifesting to them through a river or two, and perhaps multiple branches and streams. Think on this analogy.

How can you get to the invisible water source, forest dweller, if you are curious about where the life-giving streams around you come from? You could simply head for the mountains, but they're large—an entire universe as far as you're concerned. Navigating through the peaks and valleys of such mountains without a clear goal wouldn't get you very far.

You need a direct link or path to follow.

So you come across a stream that's close to you, one that was easy for you to find. This stream, like others, leads up to a branch. The branch leads up to one of a pair of rivers. The rivers merge at the water source. And at this amazing place, the waters have hewn the stone of the mountain, allowing you access.

Divinity, or the Source of the universe, is just like the font sending waters out through the surrounding lands. The Source, too, provides countless links to itself. These links represent all manner of energies, as well as how these energies are represented by the two genders of the universe. The Source is everything, after all, and any energy or concept in existence came from it.

For example, some of the links to Divinity can be male or female love and compassion, male or female protection and security, male or female nurturing, male or female aggression, male or female . . . anything, really. The ancients picked up on the fact that whatever you're concerned with, at any moment, is something that relates to our Creator. And over millennia humankind named these multiple aspects of Divinity.

These are the Gods and Goddesses, and they're all real.

All we need do is find the ones that are right for us, either for a particular phase of our development, or for a specific magickal or spiritual working. By tapping into, say, Kali's "stream," we can find our way to the Source when we are concerned, perhaps, with matters of protection, from a female perspective.

Don't think that the universe was created by thousands of independent deities, each acting on behalf of its own people or eventual followers. The Source is truly the only energy font—we just created the names and appearances for this energy's manifestations.

Then how can these names be real? They're real in the psyche of we who believe in them. A group can make up its own deity, agreeing on the energies it represents, its appearance, and its name. This constructed *godform*, through prayer and absorbed magickal energy, will then provide a real link to divinity. The name will only be a sonic link to currents of energy that were always there. By naming these currents, and identifying them with beings that have faces and forms, we simply make it easier to contact the energies.

As we'll see in part three, adding magickal energy to thoughts to lend them reality can be done on a much smaller scale, too. This is the secret of all magick, and one you'll soon master.

We won't be creating any deities as part of this book's workings, however. The Gods and Goddesses we'll be linking with have existed in the world's group mind for millennia. For a list of some nocturnal deities that I have worked with, and the energies that correspond to each, see appendix A, "Night's Gods and Goddesses."

As the appendix title implies, we'll be contacting beings that are primarily associated with dark energies—the deities that appeal more naturally to nightkind. Feel free to use these names, find other dark deities from pantheons you feel more comfortable with, or occasionally contact the male and female polarities of Divinity in more universal aspects. That is, you can often call on the "God and Goddess," relying on that point in the Source where the energies first split by gender into two major rivers of power.

The choice is yours about how to pray or make contact at any given time. There are some names I rely on for specific needs, for instance, and some, like Inanna, that I connect with often. Yet I'll often find myself praying to the God and Goddess in universal forms, too—although most often when I'm not performing a ritual.

Do consider reaching out to some of the names when you're working on a specific bit of magick or a facet of personal development. The god-forms have gathered tremendous power over the years, which is why even ceremonial mages who don't consider themselves pagan have called on these beings to accomplish amazing things in their lodges and groups.

Adding the religious love for deities that most Witches possess, however, can produce even stronger results with godform workings.

Find out now how to use simple invocation and advanced godform assumption to experience the deities, be they of light or shadow.

The Secrets of Calling Them

I'm not a big fan of armchair-theory occultism. If I teach something in one of my books or lectures, I've experienced it. And what's worked for me should work for others; I don't claim to have been born with any special gifts. So allow me again to step back into personal mode and share how I found the Gods and Goddesses of Night after having wandered away from paganism for a few years. It may help more than a few of you who had or have similar feelings of disenchantment.

Recall that I discussed a time in my life when traditional Craft ways left me feeling alienated. I then began practicing ceremonial magick without any connection to organized religion for a few years. I tried, unsuccessfully, to relate to Divinity in a nameless, faceless way.

But my magick still worked. Even the most Kabbalistic rituals and conjurations, filled with more Hebrew God names than a scholar can keep track of, worked; all this despite my never having been Jewish or having had any cultural connection to these God names. I just knew that certain ceremonial rites called on the names for years, and that the names had been called upon for years before that. I knew there was power in sticking to the built up energies these rites represented.

During my practice with and studies of the magickal systems of the world, I came across a ceremonial practice that would help me, interestingly enough, return to Witchcraft with a vigor I never imagined possible.

Magickal lodges such as the Golden Dawn often relied on a technique called godform assumption. To keep things simple, I'll say this of the practice: A mage would, through intense visualization, assume the form of a deity (usually an Egyptian one in the Golden Dawn). This practitioner would have to understand the nature of the deity and be able to visualize him or her. Then, the body of light or astral body could be shapeshifted, through visualization, to match the appearance of the God or Goddess. Acting in the form of this deity, one could perform powerful magick, related, of course, to the energies of the particular deity.

The practice began to fascinate me, although I couldn't figure out why at first. I began to enjoy deeply any rites where I assumed the form of one of the Old Gods. Always feeling free to wander outside traditional lodge workings anyway, I began experimenting with godforms of more than just the Egyptian pantheon. I began calling on the Greek Gods I knew as a child, and the Sumerian ones that I had found later on.

But only by assuming their forms—by thus intensely invoking them—did I begin to really know them. I felt a connection with Divinity that I attained no other way. And, because I was only calling on the aspects of the Source that I was seeking, I never felt uncomfortable. Although I hadn't formally identified how my nocturnal nature fit in with the Craft yet, I had found which energies and types of deities called to me and literally and figuratively spoke to me.

It seemed no accident that so many light Gods and Goddesses in the world's pantheons had dark siblings. Every type of working, mundane or magickal, has a light and dark aspect. My natural inclination to positive darkness finally found a way to express itself to the Source. I felt no need to follow the mainstream traditions anymore. I had experienced the facets and energies of the God and Goddess that worked for me.

Taking on or assuming the godform of Inanna, in particular, helped me find my place in paganism most clearly. The branch of Divinity that she represents is so powerful that the most important Goddesses of the world closely resemble her. By many names, the essence of Inanna is known.

This assumption of Inanna's form and essence taught me the secrets of true invocation, of making real contact with Divinity.

I originally designed the rite to establish contact with the other side in a ritualistic way. Using the basic principle of like attracts like, I sympathetically simulated a descent into the Underworld. In doing so, I elaborately recreated the myth of how Inanna was met at seven gates by Neti or Nergal, the guardian and husband of the Queen of the Underworld, Ereshkigal. While going through these steps, building toward a peak in the rite when the veil would be parted for me, I maintained Inanna's form as a second skin of sorts. I imagined at all times what the Goddess would have gone through in such a trek, and lived it in my imagination during the ritual.

She was with me.

Sure, I'd done invocations before. I had read words from books aloud, and tried to imagine a link being established to the Gods, but never had I felt the embrace of the Goddess so strongly as when I walked surrounded by her glowing skin. Never had I felt her within me so strongly as when I acted with her history and nature blocking out all else from my mind.

As that night progressed, certain parts of the ritual I had scripted started to no longer make sense, and some parts just vanished from my memory. I felt a new sense of purpose in performing the ritual—something more primal than just the need to succeed at a task. It was a calling I felt, a need to find a part of me that lay hidden. I went on with the ritual, modifying it through an intuition that didn't seem my own. The presence of Inanna redefined what I was setting out to accomplish.

Originally, I had planned on using the ritual to open a link to the other side—a link I could then possibly count on for repeated skrying or other afterlife communication techniques. This would be the case, as both the Inanna ritual and later a simple Anubis one I developed have acted as just such "opening" rites that you, too, can master (the Anubis ritual is in chapter 13). However, on that first attempt the Goddess had something more to show me.

The gates to the Underworld did open that day, but I never bothered to attempt contacting one of the souls residing there. I never even got a chance to use my black skrying mirror.

What awaited me was an even darker mirror.

After passing through the last gate in my ritual, I became aware of another presence in the room. It's hard to define exactly what the feeling consisted of, and I can't be sure it would feel quite the same for each person attempting such a rite. The best I can do is to call it a weight, a presence so strong that it seemed to occupy half the space in the room with its influence. Imagine a force field that doesn't have a defining border, but which instead slowly weakens the farther away from it that you move. (It's a feeling I had felt before, although that's a tale I'll save for chapter 13.)

Only after I became aware of the full weight of this energy in the room did I see what was at its center. It was the Goddess Ereshkigal, in a form that made her the dark mirror of both Inanna and myself.

I saw my features, I saw the features I had imagined to be Inanna's, and I saw more. I saw why the ancients were inspired to write of Inanna's descent. Ereshkigal in this form was the untapped dark half of life. Sure, she was one of the many deities throughout history to be attributed the role of Death or keeper of the dead, but she was so much more . . . just like Inanna or any other God or Goddess has multiple facets. At this point I wasn't seeing the aspect of Ereshkigal that would help me contact the other side—I was seeing the aspect that would help me contact *my* other side.

As I learned, a sympathetic descent to the Underworld can work either within or without. That day I needed to go within, which was why Inanna modified the rite as we performed it. I needed to reinitiate myself to a new way of looking at the ancient energies I had tried contacting before. I would travel to the gates of the afterlife later on with a rite closer to the one that I had originally written. We'll be exploring such openings of the gates and a great many other advanced workings in this book's companion volume.

Soon a great many powerful experiences will enter your life with the help of the Gods of Old. You just learned the secrets of true invocation, of contacting the primal energies and personifications of the Divine. Now we'll outline these secrets and break them out into simple but effective steps you can add to any ritual. While every rite won't require such intensity, and you won't always have time to do more than a simple invocation, godform assumption is a technique worth mastering for those times when you can call on it.

Finding Them in Legends

Before you try inviting a God or Goddess to lend energy to a ritual, learn everything you can about this deity. Not only will such research help you pick the right being for your particular need, it will also help you house him or her within your body. You cannot effectively invoke Gods and Goddesses without understanding them.

As mentioned earlier, appendix A contains many dark divinities to choose from, and gives some information about each. This is a good starting point, and for most purposes should help you establish at least some contact with a God or Goddess. However, this information is best used as something to keep in mind while performing your own exploration. You should validate any correspondences I've gathered and freely add to them.

The Gods and Goddesses we work with in Nocturnal Witchcraft fall into six general categories. They are the deities of: Night Personified, the Dark Moon, the Full Moon, Protection, Descent and Rebirth, and the Underworld.

The Lords and Ladies of Night Personified appear throughout the world's pantheons. These are beings like Nyx, associated with the enveloping ether of night in all its forms, or Hypnos, associated more with dreams. Night is the time of greatest power for Nocturnal Witches, and the states of mind associated with these hours are ones we can work with effectively. Gods of Night can help.

Ruling the Dark Moon are deities associated with banishings and other positive but destructive magick—godforms such as Hecate and Pasht. Most important to note about these beings is that banishings can be used positively for most any task—to heal or banish illness, to be rid of poverty, to destroy links to dangerous habits, and so on. The best time to contact such deities is, obviously, on the night of the Dark Moon, or the nights immediately preceding this darkest one.

Harnessing the power of the Full Moon are Nocturnal Deities representing very different energies. The energies these beings help foster are linked to fertility—to magick based on developing or drawing in a desired result rather than removing an undesired one. Interestingly, while most pantheons contain only Goddesses for the Full Moon, Sumer had a God and Goddess pair—Nanna and Ningal, respectively—attributed to this essence.

Protection is important for anyone, but can take on new dimensions for Witches of all kinds. While the Burning Times are years of horror that are fading further into the pages of history, you can't take for granted that *cowans* (the uninitiated) will understand Witchcraft or your participation in it. Add such possible antagonists to the list of traditional predators in our world, and you can see why reaching Divine protectors can be a useful practice. And the Dark Ones such as Kali and the Furies protect their children, we nightkind, most fiercely!

Gods and Goddesses who willfully descended into the Underworld to emerge changed or reborn represent a powerful paradigm that we can act upon—a dark initiation, if you will. They are wonderful to invoke when we, too, need to be brought to the brink of the unseen world, but shouldn't be used this way for just any rite. Most times, you will call on these deities for their wisdom and not to have the same experiences they did. Among the descending deities we meet Inanna, who was transformed by her dark sister Ereshkigal; we meet Kore, who changed her name to Persephone after becoming one with the other side.

The Gods that these descenders meet are the gatekeepers of the Underworld. We will be speaking more of such deities, like Anubis and Ereshkigal, in chapter 13. As we'll see, these beings should not be invoked for just any magickal rite. These energies can only be applied for workings that deal with the afterlife.

If a deity appeals to you or perhaps resonates with you on some level, you should seek out as much additional information about him or her as you can find. Even if you don't have a ritual in mind right now, this God or Goddess might have some personal significance to you that's worth investigating.

How do you learn more about said God or Goddess? Check out a few books on mythology that contain tales of him or her. Sometimes, only reading the stories of deities can help you to truly know them. And this goes for more than just the ones I mention in appendix A. You may need to find other Gods and Goddesses that speak best to you, through myth. Much as you would get to know a recurring character in a series of novels, spend some time seeing how a particular aspect of Divinity behaved in a few legends.

Speaking of characters in novels, note that for the most part myths are not fleshed out in books using the type of prose found in modern novels. A product of their times, myths are told, not shown. Doubtless, you'll notice right away that certain storytelling techniques were lacking in centuries past. This is not necessarily a bad thing, either.

First, in myths there's rarely a blow-by-blow description of even the most exciting events. For instance, major battles at the climax of a legend are often summed up with lines such as "Theseus slew the Minotaur." This is beneficial for those of us reading a myth for religious purposes. The minimal action details help keep the tales short enough to digest in quantity, letting you devour most myths about a particular God or Goddess in an evening.

Another beneficial aspect of myths is that they do not let you into the minds of their players. Myths often portray the actions of mortals and deities as if the writer were a fly observing them from a temple wall. This lack of viewpoint eliminates the chance that too many modern opinions might have seeped into a retelling of an ancient tale. After all, you're interested in an overview of what energies the ancients felt were attributed to a particular God or Goddess, and not the motivations that some translator or editor over the years might have believed the Gods felt.

Note the opening lines of the introduction to what is perhaps the most famous collection of myths, *Bullfinch's Mythology*: "The religions of ancient Greece and Rome are extinct. The so-called divinities of Olympus have not a single worshipper among living men. They belong now not to the department of theology, but to those of literature and taste." I know that more than a few people reading this would object! Look for the cosmic attributes presented in myths, and not the modern opinions and drama that some writers feel the need to inject into them. Fortunately, in the case of Thomas Bullfinch, the majority of the myths in his book escape such editorials.

While reading your chosen myths, take simple notes. Jot down the themes and actions that seem to recur in a deity's legends. Perhaps you might want to copy some of the information in appendix A into a notebook, and then add or cross out data as it applies to your purpose (some aspects of a deity are not applicable to every ritual). At the very least, appendix A will help you know some of the themes to look for as you read. Don't take my energy correspondences on faith. See what the ancients had to say about a God or Goddess. See why they attributed, say, the power of dark magick to Hecate. Search out on your own some examples of why the God or Goddess of your interest is associated with certain energies.

True Invocation

Once you've read all you can about a deity, and compiled your own notes and attributes, you will need to apply the knowledge you've gained in two ways: as an aid to writing invocations, and as a mental aid while assuming a godform (more on this in a moment).

Having gathered some specific data about a particular God or Goddess, you will find that writing an invocation to him or her is easier than you thought. Some books even take care of this step for you, and that's fine as long as the findings of the author mesh well with the view of the deity that you have built up through your own reading. Feel free to modify published invocations to reflect any aspects of a deity you sense are not well represented in the words. In this book, there are only a few examples of invocations, to allow room for all the techniques we need to cover.

Make certain that your invocation, be it original, copied, or rewritten, contains as many of the specifics about a deity as possible. The more notes you take, the more information you'll have to choose from. Don't set out to write the most poetic invocation possible, torturing yourself over every line. Unless you form a Nocturnal Coven (more on this later) only two beings will ever hear the invocation. And if you do work with others, feel free to let them add to the invocation.

However it is compiled, the invocation must do three things:

1. identify the deity;
2. state the reason he or she is needed; and
3. invite him or her in.

You identify the deity through attribute listing, just like you'll find the ancients did. Then you explain how you seek help in one of the areas that fall under the deity's expertise or domain. Finally, you ask the deity to be with you to provide this help. Here's a short example of how following these three steps would result in an effective invocation of Hecate:

> *Queen of the dark sky, be with me this night.*
> *Cunning mistress of dark magicks, be with me this night.*
> *I seek your aid in ridding myself of this harmful influence.*
> *I seek your strength in banishing all power that*
> *(insert bad influence name) has over me.*
> *Grant me time to bask in your caress.*
> *Be with me this night.*

Can you see how the invocation was written with the three steps in mind? Sure, they're mixed and repeated in various forms, but they're there. Remembering the three steps makes it possible to create effective invocations with little effort. They need only be long enough to establish who the deity is in your mind, and why you need to contact him or her at this time.

Such words you craft will help you find that spark of Divinity within yourself. We contain a sympathetic link to the Gods at all times. Proper invocation helps us focus on the part of this link we need at any given moment.

For quick rites or a circle cast for prayer, reading this type of invocation aloud will suffice. This is what I refer to as "simple invocation." However, there will be times when you want more power added to a ritual. If you want to maximize the effect of calling on the Gods, you should use a godform assumption—dare I call this true invocation?

Godforms

You get out of a ritual what you put into it. And most rites need a significant amount of power. You cannot perform magick by only going through the motions, so to speak. You have to add energy or power to your words and actions in any ritual—with invocations it's a matter of giving what you'll ultimately receive. That is, although you need to expel some of your own power to make them work, effective invocations will bring the power of a God or Goddess to a ritual.

And one of the most effective ways to empower an invocation or any other magickal act is through visualization and concentration.

The knowledge you gather to write an invocation can be applied to generating power through visualization. While reading myths and legends associated with a God or Goddess, you develop a better sense of the being's personality and possible appearance. Let this image ferment in your unconsciousness—you'll be using it during the calling.

You should also try to come up with correspondences for a deity that make sense to you. For Hecate I like to have a rough old piece of obsidian, to remind me of how her wisdom is ancient and dark throughout; I also use a dried-up rose to remind me of how she works to corrode things to maintain a permanently pleasing situation. But that's just my symbolism. The only correspondences that will work for you, however, are the ones you're inspired to use after having read some myths. You need to determine which sympathetic energies to have present at your calling to make the room and your own aura more receptive to the deity. If a sacred plant is mentioned for the deity in a myth (or if you come across such a correspondence elsewhere that makes sense to you), put it in a vase on your altar. Or, burn this plant—dried, first—as an incense (you can also just use one of the nocturnal scents listed in appendix B).

The idea of setting up the room like this isn't to appease the Gods so they'll see fit to grace you with their presence. All you're doing is making sure your mind will more easily be able to sympathetically link with the specific current of our Creator that you're reaching out to. Don't worry if you're using a particular incense for no other reason than that you think Hecate, for instance, would like it. If you believe it makes sense to use a particular correspondence, your subconscious mind will gladly use that as an aid to attaining ritual consciousness.

Now, with preparations out of the way, we can return to the image of the God or Goddess you've been building. Before actually reading the invocation within a ritual setting and a nocturnal circle (explained in the next chapter), you will need to make clear in your mind your vision of the deity. The trick here is to let your intuition guide you. You will likely pick up on various images while reading about the deity in myths. Let these features come to you when you're preparing. Hair and eye color, manner of dress, voice, even posture—whatever aspects stand out in your mind should be trusted as inspired visions. Build an amalgam of them.

Know that whatever form you select or create is the absolute correct form to work with. This is the form your subconscious, magickal mind will understand as being the best way to link to the deity.

Consider again our example of Hecate. When reading about her I found myself imagining an older but still alluring woman, with a voice that has a subtle accent but an intense, imperious tone. Black and gray multilayered robes make up her garb of choice, in my mind.

When you have a form selected and firmly in place in your mind's eye, you will have to assimilate this image in a way you've done before . . . when thinking of yourself. Have you ever imagined yourself with a different haircut or wearing a different outfit? You will have to be able to see the godform you've built as a kind of outfit and makeover in your mind's eye. While invoking, you will have to *know* that you resemble the deity. Then, during the ritual, you will need to imagine that you are wearing the God or Goddess image as a second skin.

Again, like attracts like. By having correspondences in the room that are related to the deity, the room is made ready to welcome the energy you're seeking. By having a knowledge of the deity in the forefront of your mind, you prepare your body to house the God or Goddess in much the same way. During the invocation itself, you will welcome the visualized form of the God or Goddess to your inner temple.

Now, for the how-to that ties all the aforementioned elements together.

Assuming a Godform

When you reach the point in your circle casting when the God or Goddess needs to be called (see the next chapter), stand behind the altar and prepare yourself. Do so by reflecting on what you hope to accomplish through the complete ritual. Think about the aspects of the deity you've chosen to work with. Why is he or she appropriate to your working? The point here is to remind yourself, before you begin, of your intent. Concentrating on intent should precede any magick to help you focus on the particular energies you plan on using.

Try to simplify the essence of the deity to a word or two, such as "protection" or "peace and healing." Repeat the chosen phrase silently and close your eyes. Continuing your silent mantra, tilt your head up and raise your arms, palms to the ceiling or sky.

Keep your eyes closed and imagine a glowing silver maelstrom above you, shining in the darkness. See it as a whirlpool of cosmic light, much like a spiral galaxy would appear in a powerful telescope. However, this spiral is more like a cone, with its arms connected at a luminous point far above you. The other ends of these trailing streams of light spread around you and sink into the ground below, somewhere off on the horizon. It is a slowly moving vortex of divine energy you're beholding.

Continue to silently repeat the phrase you chose. As you do so, fix your attention on one of the spiraling arms. The one you choose in this seemingly random way is the right one, have no doubt. See the arm begin to apparently grow in size. No, that's not right . . . what is actually happening? Is it moving down toward you?

Straightening itself out gracefully, the spiral arm becomes a silver beam approaching the top of your head. Feel its pulsing energy approaching you.

Contact. When the beam reaches you, repeat your chosen phrase one last time, in acknowledgment that this aspect of Divine energy has just touched you. Relish for a moment the slight jolt you may feel.

While taking a deep breath, begin to slowly lower your arms. The idea here is to feel and imagine—with eyes closed—that the energy is entering you gradually from the top of your head as you perform this action. On your first inhalation, you should lower your arms to about shoulder level (so they're pointing straight out at your sides). Feel the energy reach your shoulders. As you exhale, feel its pulsing in your head, neck, and shoulders increase in intensity.

Take in another breath and lower your arms to forty-five-degree angles, feeling and seeing the energy lowering to your hips. Exhale, letting the energy pulse stronger now down through this area.

Finally, take in a third breath, lowering your arms to your sides and imagining the energy moving down to your feet. On your final exhalation while concentrating in such a way, feel and visualize the energy pulsing through your entire body.

Concentrate on your link to this particular Divine energy current for a moment longer. See once again where the beam enters the top of your head. See your entire body glowing with this silver light. Be aware of your new aura or body of light.

Open your eyes. You should feel as if you are in a slightly altered state of awareness, which is a result of more than just the visualizations and mantra you have performed. It's a result of the Divine power you have tapped. Use this altered state to proceed—know you are now close to the Divine.

Look at any symbols you have gathered in honor of the God or Goddess you are about to invoke. Do not meditate on them. Rather, trust your subconscious to understand the significance the symbols have to your working.

Here you will begin to either recite or read the invocation you have prepared. Having written or modified the words, you should feel the full impact of their meaning resonate in your mind automatically. This is desirable, as you'll be doing more than just reading or reciting here.

As you slowly voice the invocation, begin to imagine, with your eyes open, that the glowing silver aura is morphing around you. Recall the type of visualization you perform when imagining yourself with a different haircut or outfit. Use this to now imagine your aura changing to resemble the form of the God or Goddess.

While the pacing of it is not crucial, the process of godform assumption works easiest if you gradually visualize the changes as you recite the invocation. Try to see the general changes first and then focus on each detail. It's kind of like molding a figure from clay. First you establish the anthropomorphic form, then you mold the rough clothing outline, then you add specifics such as belts and accessories. Then, when you're really warmed up, you can work on the face.

But feel free to visualize the aspects of your inspired godform in whatever sequence works best for you.

When you finish reciting the words, close your eyes to put the finishing touches on your visualization. Some of you who are newer to visualization may prefer to not add color to the godform just yet. If you're comfortable with visualization, however, feel free to add details like actual hair, eye, and, say, robe color. (Incidentally, there are some shortcuts for boosting overall visualization ability given in part two.)

You are now clothed and permeated with the form of the God or Goddess. You can act from this point on in the ritual with his or her power aiding you. Don't worry about visualizing the silver link to the top of your forehead any longer. Just maintain as well as you can the visualization of the godform surrounding you as you perform your magick.

When the rite is ended, you will want to return to normal waking consciousness. Announce out loud that the rite has ended and offer your thanks to the God or Goddess for lending his or her aid. Please do not "dismiss" him or her as if you were letting an employee go home. This is an aspect of the Creator we're talking about here!

After offering thanks, close your eyes and visualize the godform slowly morphing back into the silver glowing aura. When all you can imagine once again is light, you'll be ready to properly channel this energy. With each exhalation, imagine it beginning to dissipate, turning into a mistlike substance as it leaves the pores of your skin. Some of it will, through this osmosis process, leave you and return to the Source. Some of it will stay with you, providing quite a nice high for the rest of the night.

Let's now look at the ritual structure within which you'll make such calls to Divinity, and perform your dark miracle working.

Chapter Four
Circles of Night and Lunar Light

A place that can be called nowhere yet can reach everywhere; an instant that stands outside of time yet can affect all of it . . . magick circles are cast to become just such mysterious wonders and help accomplish wondrous things.

In ancient times, pagans could worship and perform their rites in consecrated temples and sacred groves. Today it is necessary, before each rite, to sanctify the area where we plan to work. Whether you wish to clear the area of negativity before meditating or training, or need to create a full circle for a celebration or spellcasting, you will find in this chapter a way to create sacred space for each instance.

You'll be using both the banishing and nocturnal magick circles regularly in your practice, but don't worry too much about memorizing them. You can use them straight from the book at first—they'll seep into your mind on their own.

Also in this chapter are simple celebration rites for Dark and Full Moons. Like other rituals, these are to be performed after the nocturnal circle is cast. By attuning with these absolute-phase nights in the moon's cycle you will greatly speed up your progress through the techniques revealed in parts two and three.

Banishing, Training

The power of thought is immense and can accomplish much good, or harm, depending on who is wielding it. Negativity, in particular, has a nasty way of lingering in a place. Those with even slight psychic sensitivity find it uncomfortable to walk through a room where there was an argument, for instance.

To ensure your own psychic experiences and training sessions are distraction free, you'll want to quickly clear your surroundings of any counteractive energy that might have built up in a room. Indeed, this is how you'll use banishings for now. With a little practice, however, the banishing technique revealed here can be modified to rid a space or person of focused, harmful energies.

To perform a simple "training" banishing, you'll need nothing but the power of your mind. You can set up your nocturnal altar if you wish, but none of the tools will be required to perform the banishing itself. You could make use of the altar candles, however, as you'll want to turn off electric lights and perform the rite by candlelight, if possible.

The Banishing

Stand in the center of the space you wish to cleanse and take three deep breaths.

Close your eyes and imagine that you are standing between two spheres of energy: one is above you, one below. The one above is pulsing and silver. The sphere below you is the earth; see it in its entirety as a black sphere, to avoid distraction.

Sense how the crackling, silver light from above seeks to rain down upon the earth, where it can be absorbed by the black sphere. Feel this charged potential slipping around you, almost like a pulsing drizzle, and see the energy falling as brief sparks.

Keeping your eyes closed, imagine that you are growing in height. You are moving up to meet the silver sphere, although your feet are firmly grounded on the absorbing sphere below you.

Raise both arms and touch the crackling energy above you. Take one deep breath and feel the silver light enter your hands.

Open your eyes and exhale as you lower your arms. Feel the energy move through you, following the descending height of your hands. Finish your exhalation with your hands in front of your chest. Form two crescents, thumbs up and fingers down, that face each other. Each finger should be touching its opposite counterpart. Were someone to stand in front of you, it would look as if you were holding a small invisible ball against your chest, with curled fingers underneath.

Inhale again, feeling more energy come down through your head and body to chest level. Exhale, imagining the energy coalescing inside your chest as a tiny silver sphere.

Inhale, letting your hands move apart. Feel more energy come down to the sphere at your chest.

Exhale, moving your hands down lower and imagining that the power is passing down through your legs and into your feet.

Slowly inhale and exhale three more times. With each inhalation, feel the power course down through your body. With each exhalation, imagine the sphere in your chest growing brighter, as it is drawing on some of the energy passing all the way through you.

For your next three slow breath cycles, imagine the sphere growing to fill the room, bisecting the floor at its equator. That is, when you've finished expanding the ball you should imagine that half the sphere is underneath you and the room, while the other half is like a dome over you. Pull energy down with each inhalation; imagine the silver sphere expanding with each exhalation. You decide how large an area you want to clear of negativity, and scale each of the three expansions accordingly. For instance, to banish negativity from a nine-foot circle, grow the sphere to three, then six, then nine feet on the first, second, then third exhalations.

Close your eyes and reinforce your visualization, breathing normally. Feel the room pulsing with the energy you drew down. You are surrounded by a silver sphere in which no negativity can exist.

Remain in the giant energy sphere for as long as you wish. There's no need to "close" this cleansed space when you decide to leave the room. The sphere is made of borrowed energy that will naturally dissipate on its own, leaving behind all its positive effects. Notice I never asked you to imagine yourself shrinking back to normal size. This subtle alteration to your way of thinking reinforces your domination over any lesser and less desirable energies that once resided around you.

Practice this simple banishing often. Once you've gotten the hang of it, it should take only two or three minutes to effectively perform. I recommend doing it before you go to sleep, and before you perform any kind of psychic training. You should also use the simple banishing before you cast a full nocturnal circle.

Casting the Nocturnal Circle

With the exception of simple meditations and psychic exercises, all other mystical workings should be performed inside a properly cast circle. While the banishing creates cleansed space, the nocturnal circle creates sacred space. It is within nocturnal circles that you'll best be able to commune with the God and Goddess. It is within this magickal area that you'll best be able to alter reality.

Before you begin, make sure you have everything you need for the working at hand—this includes whatever you plan on accomplishing once the circle is cast. The altar should be set up as described in chapter 2. Note that when you cast the nocturnal circle for the first time, you will not have any consecrated tools. A simple tool dedication is taught in the next section of this chapter (along with a dedication for yourself). However, you'll have to cast your first circle without the help of an athame. For this one circle, replace all mention of an athame with the pointer and middle fingers of the appropriate hand. You can then perform the dedication and use the athame to close the circle.

When preparing the room, leave a little treat for yourself in a corner, out of the space where your circle will be cast. This treat can be a small piece of cake and cup of juice or alcohol, depending on your age, of course. You'll partake in this food and drink after the rite to relax and ground yourself.

The room should be dark, lighted only by the two black or silver altar candles (do not light the elemental fire candle yet). Make sure your tools are oriented so that when you stand with the altar before you, you are facing east, the direction of elemental air and the powers of mind.

If you wish to take a ritual bath before putting on your magickal garments, do so. This can be a simple bath by candlelight where you reflect on what you hope to accomplish this particular night.

One note before proceeding: The casting mentions skrying several times, calling on you to actually try and see the energies and even the beings that manifest. If you haven't developed skrying abilities yet (see chapter 6 for how to skry various dark surfaces and portals), do your best to sense or imagine the energies at each point for now. Your circle castings will only become more intense when you add true skrying later.

The Nocturnal Circle

1. Perform the banishing while facing east, with the altar before you.
2. Lift your athame with your projecting hand—the hand you write with—and hold it blade up. With the pommel (the part of the handle that's sticking out from the bottom of your fist), knock three times lightly on your altar.
3. Walk clockwise (around the left side of your altar) to the easternmost edge of what will be your magick circle (this should correspond with the circumference of the sphere from your banishing). Point the athame blade at the floor.

4. Try to summon the feeling you had as the energy was coursing through you during the banishing. It helps to slightly tense your muscles. Feel your body tingling as it did when you were calling down energy and imagine this energy seeping out of your hand and athame blade. At first you'll sense only trickles coming out; wait a moment and imagine the power building in intensity until it comes out resembling a silver laser beam in your mind's eye. With your eyes open you should visualize this energy cutting through the air and connecting with the edge of your cleansed space. Think of it as a laser sword with a point that you'll be dragging around the floor of the room.

5. Move clockwise around the room visualizing the blade of light leaving a glowing trail behind it. Imagine, as clearly as you can, that you are drawing a circle of silver light as you walk around the room. Connect the line when you come to the east once again, completing the circle.

6. Move clockwise around the altar to your original spot facing east with the altar before you. Close your eyes and strengthen your visualization of the silver circle. See it blazing against an inky background. See how the darkness on both sides of the circle coexists with the silver slice. The darkness forms a tangible pressure that keeps the circle in place, much as air keeps an inflated balloon from either collapsing or exploding outward.

7. Open your eyes and put your athame down onto the altar. Pick up the elemental air incense stick with your projecting hand. Light it using one of the altar candles and blow on it to get it smoking. Move around the left side of the altar to the east quarter of your circle.

8. Facing out to the east, use the stick of incense to trace a large elemental air invoking pentagram (see figure 4-1 on page 65) in the air, about chest level. Imagine it glowing yellow as you do so. To charge the glowing construct fully, tense your muscles to raise up energy as you did to cast the circle. Take a deep breath, feeling the energy course through you. Exhale, pushing energy out of your projecting hand and

into the pentagram. See, as best as you can, the pentagram glowing brighter yellow.

9. Extend and raise your projecting arm, the one holding the incense, above the floating pentagram. Look through the pentagon at the glyph's center—peer through it into the darkness. While gazing this way, say:

> *Forces of air, elementals of the east, emerge from the black of night.*
> *In honor of the Old Ones, come and lend your power to my rite.*

Allow yourself to skry for a moment through the pentagon center. Try to see what comes forth from the shadows.

10. Walk clockwise around the edge of circle, letting the incense smoke purify it. State your purpose by saying:

> *I purify with air.*

Finish at the east and move clockwise to return to your starting point at the altar. Place the incense in the censer for now.

11. Pick up the fire candle, light it using one of the altar candles, and move clockwise around your altar to the south quarter of the circle.

12. Facing south, use the lit candle to slowly draw a red fire invoking pentagram (see figure 4-1) in the air. Charge the pentagram as you did in the east by raising energy and pushing it out of your projecting hand. See the pentagram glowing brighter red.

13. Extend your arm, raising the candle above the floating pentagram. Peer into the darkness through the red pentagon at the glyph's center. While skrying, say:

> *Forces of fire, elementals of the south, emerge from the black of night.*
> *In honor of the Old Ones, come and lend your power to my rite.*

Gaze through the pentagon center, again trying to see what emerges from the shadows.

14. Walk clockwise around the edge of the circle, retracing it with the lit fire candle. Say:

> *I purify with fire.*

Finish at the south, then move clockwise to return to your starting point at the altar. Blow out the fire candle (it's not for a spell, so it's okay to do so). You will be able to use this candle for a few more circle castings.

15. Lift the water cup with your projecting hand, and pivot clockwise so that you can arrive at the west quarter of the circle.

16. Facing west, use the cup of water to slowly draw a blue water invoking pentagram (see figure 4-1) before you. Charge the pentagram by raising energy and pushing it out of your projecting hand. See the pentagram glowing brighter blue.

17. Extend your arm, raising the cup above the floating pentagram. Peer into the darkness through the blue pentagon at the center, saying:

    Forces of water, elementals of the west, emerge from the black of night.
    In honor of the Old Ones, come and lend your power to my rite.

    Gaze through the pentagon center until satisfied your call has been heard.

18. Switch the water cup to your other hand. Use your projecting hand to sprinkle drops onto the floor as you walk clockwise around the edge of the circle. Say:

    I purify with water.

    Finish at the west, then turn clockwise to return to your starting point behind the altar. Place the water cup on the altar.

19. Pick up the salt container with your projecting hand, and move clockwise a few steps to come to the north quarter.

20. Facing north, use the salt container to slowly draw a green earth invoking pentagram (see figure 4-1). Raise energy and charge the pentagram. See it glowing brighter green.

21. Extend your arm, raising the salt container above the floating pentagram. Peer through the green pentagon at the center, saying:

    Forces of earth, elementals of the north, emerge from the black of night.
    In honor of the Old Ones, come and lend your power to my rite.

    Skry for a few moments.

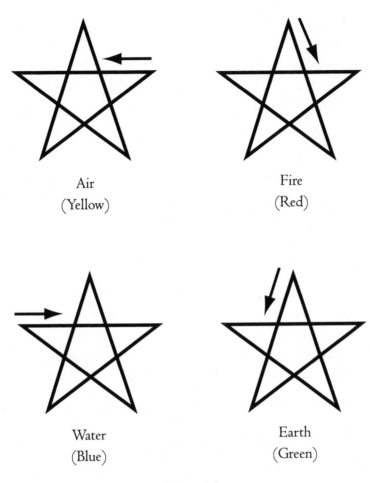

Air
(Yellow)

Fire
(Red)

Water
(Blue)

Earth
(Green)

Figure 4-1

22. Switch the salt container to your other hand. Use your projecting hand to scatter pinches of salt onto the floor as you walk clockwise around the circle. Say:

I purify with earth.

Finish at the north. Move clockwise around the altar to return to your starting point. Place the salt container on the altar.

23. If you're planning to use the air incense for your ritual, leave it burning in the censer. Otherwise, quickly dip the stick into the cup of water, and light at this time the incense that you will use for the remainder of the rite.

24. Lift the athame with your projecting hand and trace a silver invoking pentagram (starting at the top, like an earth pentagram) over your nocturnal portal. See this glyph blazing over the portal, representing the hidden energy in a Dark Moon, in the night, and in your very being. Let the glyph fade as you begin to skry the portal. While gazing, say:

    The nocturnal circle is cast. I now stand in sacred space.
    I am between worlds, surrounded by eternal night. So mote it be.

    Continue to skry if any visions present themselves.

25. When you are ready, invoke Divine aid to your rite. If you are doing a ritual for a serious need, you will want to assume the godform of a particular God or Goddess as described in chapter 3. For quick workings, a spoken request for their aid and presence—simple invocation—will do.

26. Perform whatever magickal working you have planned. This could be a spell, a celebration or moon rite, or even an intense time of communion with the God or Goddess you've invoked (especially if you've assumed one of their forms).

27. When your ritual task is complete, give thanks to the God and Goddess for helping you. If you did a godform assumption, allow that form to dissipate (as described in chapter 3).

28. Pick up your athame with your projecting hand. Walk around the left of the altar to the east.

29. Extend your arm, holding up the athame, and say:

    Forces of air, beings of the east, many thanks for lending energy to my rite.
    Retreat now to the shadows with the blessings
    of the God and Goddess of Night.

Air
(Yellow)

Fire
(Red)

Water
(Blue)

Earth
(Green)

Figure 4-2

Draw a yellow banishing air pentagram (see figure 4-2) with the
athame. Maintain the visualization for a moment, then move to
the south.

30. Hold up the athame and say:

Forces of fire, beings of the south, many thanks for lending energy to my rite.
Retreat now to the shadows with the blessings
of the God and Goddess of Night.

Draw a red banishing fire pentagram (see figure 4-2) with the athame. See the blazing glyph, and move to the west quarter of the circle.

31. Extend your arm and say:

    Forces of water, beings of the west, many thanks for lending energy to my rite.
    Retreat now to the shadows with the blessings
    of the God and Goddess of Night.

    Draw a blue banishing water pentagram (see figure 4-2) with the athame. Maintain the visualization, then move to the north.

32. Hold up the athame and say:

    Forces of earth, beings of the north, many thanks for lending energy to my rite.
    Retreat now to the shadows with the blessings
    of the God and Goddess of Night.

    Draw a green banishing earth pentagram (see figure 4-2) with the athame. See the blazing symbol, and move clockwise to the east quarter of the circle.

33. Facing east, switch the athame to your receiving hand (likely your left). Look down and make a cutting motion, thereby slicing through the energy field of the circle.

34. Point the athame at the circle and walk counterclockwise. See the silver energy moving back up into the blade. Go completely around the circle, returning to the east.

35. Move counterclockwise to end up at your starting point with the altar before you. Tap the pommel of the athame three times on the altar, still using your receiving hand, and say:

    The rite is ended, the nocturnal circle is open.
    May my will be carried through the night.

36. If you still feel the room is not quite "balanced" yet, perform another banishing at this point. Otherwise, turn on the lights.

37. Go to the cake and drink that have been lurking in the shadows outside your circle. These are charged with balanced, nocturnal forces and will help ground and return you to normal consciousness. Enjoy.

Oh, and if your little treats are gone, don't worry. They went to something in the shadows that needed them more. Chances are this will only happen outdoors, but who knows. . . .

Simple Dedications

As mentioned earlier, the first time you cast the nocturnal circle, use your pointer and middle fingers as an athame. Go through the casting in this fashion all the way through step twenty-five. Then your working, or step twenty-six, should be the following:

Dedicating Tools

Pick up in your two upturned palms the tool you wish to dedicate (your athame, at the very least, although you can even dedicate jewelry if you wish). Hold the object in front of the nocturnal portal.

Angle your hands so you can see the object's reflection in your skrying tool. See how it is surrounded by a charged, glowing darkness (this is not a contradiction of terms—more on this "less-dark darkness" when we discuss skrying setups in chapter 6).

Still looking into the portal, imagine that the nocturnal energy around the object is slowly seeping into the physical form. Feel this happening at all sides of the object; feel the energy moving around your hands (but keep your eyes on the portal). Say:

> *I dedicate you, creature of metal (or whatever material it's made of) to the*
> *service of the Gods and Goddesses of Night. Move through the shadows*
> *and be one with the darkness. So mote it be.*

Pass the object through the censer's smoke for a silent count of three.

Never use the object for mundane purposes again. Keep it wrapped in black silk if possible—or at least black cloth—until it is needed for ritual.

You can sanctify as many tools as you wish to with this rite. On your first circle casting, you'll also want to dedicate . . . yourself.

Perform the following simple rite next:

Your Dedication to Night

Place both palms on the altar and kneel before it.

Spend a moment feeling a connection with your altar, your circle's center of power. Your palms may start tingling as soon as they touch the altar cloth.

Slowly move closer to the nocturnal portal until you can see your reflection (if the portal is set up properly for skrying, you'll have to get quite close to see your face).

Meditate for a moment on how you can see yourself coexisting with the glowing darkness around you, and on what this means to you at this point in your life. Remind yourself why you feel most comfortable surrounded by night.

Gazing into the reflection of your eyes, which will look dark, like mini skrying mirrors, say:

I now cast my lot with the shadows. May the Gods and Goddesses of Night hear my words and welcome me into their embrace. So mote it be.

Move your face back from the portal, seeing it blend more with the darkness.

Lift your hands and wave some of the incense smoke into your face (don't breathe deeply at this point). Close your eyes and be aware of the mystical scent.

Open your eyes, stand up, and close the circle using steps twenty-seven and on. Do perform another banishing when the circle is undone, to see how different the energy-based process will now feel.

Remember, this isn't a full initiation. Rather, it's a way to help keep you on track as you develop your skills and your connection to the Gods of Night.

Now on to the Dark and Full Moon rites. Prepare to attune with lunar currents that will boost your powers of perception and speed your mastery of nocturnal magick.

Celebrating the Dark Moon

When seeking to access dark energies, look no further than the time of the Dark Moon. Nocturnal power is at its peak on this night, when the moon is fully blanketed by shadow.

Some of the workings in this book will have their best effects during the Dark Moon, and these will be indicated accordingly. But remember, you don't have to have a particular magickal need to recognize or celebrate this powerful phase of the moon, or the Full Moon either, for that matter.

You should celebrate as many Dark and Full phases as possible to fully experience the range of nocturnal powers available. And the celebrations don't take long; as you'll see, the rites are short. However, the effects on your development are long lasting.

To attune with the Dark Moon, set up your altar as normal. Be sure to use black candles, not silver. For incense you can use any nocturnal scent (see appendix B). Doing the rite outdoors would be best, but if this is not possible, just make sure to go outside and at least spot the Dark Moon once before beginning.

Dark Moon Rite

Perform the circle casting through step twenty-four.

Before performing step twenty-five (the invocation), turn your attention to the black candle on the right of the altar and say the following:

Behold, the only light on this night comes from within my dark circle.

Look to the left candle and say:

And the light I've set also draws in the darkness,
never seeking to fully burn it away.

Let your gaze drift either up to the moon or down to your nocturnal portal, if you're indoors. Stare at the moon for a moment, or visualize it in the portal as you saw it earlier. Think about how it is a noticeable sphere of darkness in an even inkier sky.

Now invoke a God or Goddess associated with the Dark Moon (see appendix A). You don't need to pick names if you're only planning to do a simple invocation; your choice of a specific deity is only necessary if you are doing a full godform assumption.

When your chosen form of invocation is complete, see if you feel the need to act on any God- or Goddess-inspired acts. If not, say:

The sweet light of the moon holds no sway tonight over the dark energies around me.
In the name of (God or Goddess whom you've invoked), I seek a better connection with nocturnal mysteries.

If you're outdoors, you may wish to skry the disk of the moon or any other dark region of the night (see chapter 6 for how to skry . . . anything). Indoors, your nocturnal portal will do nicely. After you've skryed, or instead of doing so, you can perform any rite that is best done during the Dark Moon.

Start the process of closing the circle with step twenty-seven.

After you ground yourself with the treats you've left, write in a journal any insights you may have received about what this night means to your development. You may be surprised at what comes through.

Now on to when lunar energies dominate the night.

By the Full Moon's Light

As we explored in chapter 2, the moon is the one object that works with the dark hours, reflecting light into them or, for a few nights, sinking into shadow. The moon's increasing light is a sympathetic link that brings very specific types of energies into our lives on a monthly basis.

Certain rituals, such as ones for prosperity or fertility, are best performed on the Full Moon. But even if you don't have such a working to do, you should still seek to commune with the lunar Gods and Goddesses on any Full Moon that you can.

For the Full Moon celebration, set up your altar as normal. If possible, you may want to use silver candles, to help signify the importance of the night. Frankincense or sandalwood make a good choice for incense, but you can use any scent that you enjoy working with.

Like the Dark Moon rite, this one is best performed outdoors. Also like that rite, if you have to do the Full Moon celebration indoors, be sure to go outside and at least spot the moon first.

Full Moon Rite

Perform the circle casting through step twenty-four.

Look at the silver candle on the right of the altar and say:

> *Behold how the light in my dark circle adds to that of the Full Moon.*

Turn to the left candle and say:

> *Yet I also draw in the lunar glow, seeking its aid.*
> *Seeking to know its mistress and master.*

Slowly turn your head up to stare at the moon if you're outdoors; if indoors, look down at your nocturnal portal. Gaze at the Full Moon for a moment or visualize it in the portal. Meditate on how the Full Moon reflects light upon us without vanquishing the night. Think about how at this time, the maximum amount of daylight is being converted to energy that is more conducive to beautiful nights.

Invoke now your choice of God or Goddess associated with the Full Moon (see appendix A). Specific names are not important if you only plan to do a minor invocation; they are extremely important, of course, if you are doing an actual godform assumption.

When you have finished your invocation or godform assumption, see if you are inspired to act on the will of the Old Ones. Perhaps a rite may come to you, perhaps a bit of advice for your endeavors. The moon deities can be quite nurturing.

Unless the God and Goddess carry the ritual in a totally different direction, say:

The light of prosperity and bounty shines upon me on this night. In the name of (God or Goddess whom you've invoked), I seek a better connection with lunar powers and inspiration.

If you're outdoors, you may wish to gaze at the moon to see if any ideas come to you. If you're inside, look back to the left silver candle. When you feel ready, you can perform a rite that is best done during the Full Moon, assuming you have one to do.

Start the process of closing the circle with step twenty-seven.

After you ground yourself with the treats, write in a journal about any insights you may have received regarding what this night means to your development.

And with these rites covered, we are ready to move on to part two—on to where we'll explore the unique psychic abilities that the night will soon impart to you.

Part Two

Mind Powers After Dark

Chapter Five
The Inner Quiet

The powers of the mind are at the core of all magick. Make no mistake about this—just reading words from a book or even a parchment won't make anything happen. Incantations and other aspects of ritual are only parts of a psychodrama that attempts to tap the unused parts of your mind. This is something I can't reinforce enough.

The best way to get the psychodrama of ritual to work for you, therefore, is to train your mind to be receptive to requests for access to its hidden regions and potential. Here's where those of you working in the shadows have an edge.

One of the biggest advantages to practicing magick primarily by night is that you can take advantage of the psychic quiet hours. As the darkness overtakes a region, more and more people begin to relax and eventually go to sleep. They're not actively generating all the psychic "interference" found during the day; they're not expending mental energy to solve problems and perform necessary tasks in, for instance, the business world.

You can feel the change that occurs at night easily for yourself. Just step out well after dark and listen. Depending on where you live, you'll notice immediately that it's quiet. That's a given. Even in New York City it's at least somewhat quieter at night.

But extend your awareness beyond just sound and you'll find something else. At first you won't be able to pinpoint exactly what you're feeling, or feeling the lack of, but it should still be obvious that something is different.

Step outside during the hours of three to five in the morning, and you'll feel it even stronger.

But you need not stay up quite that late, or get up that early, to take advantage of night's distraction-free psychic time. This chapter contains simple exercises that, when performed any time after dark, will rapidly begin to create change in your mental faculties. Start with these techniques, using the dark hours to improve your basic abilities. Then move on to rites that let you use the dark hours to create miracles.

Calming the Chaos

Before you can access those inner regions of the mind, you have to quiet the inner chaos that normally accompanies waking thought. I mentioned how this happens in others at nighttime, resulting in a clear psychic field, if you will, in the atmosphere. Make sure that you take full advantage of this time by clearing your mind as much as possible of distractions.

The first step to achieving the inner quiet, therefore, is to relax. A calm body helps induce a calm mental state. To this end, you should perform a simple deep relaxation technique. If possible, do the following after performing a banishing. Make certain the room is as dark as possible.

Deep Relaxation

Sit on a hard-backed chair, feet flat on the floor and palms down on your legs.

Close your eyes. Take a deep breath while tightening every muscle in your face that you can. Purse your lips, squint, and really squeeze every cell possible. Then hold the breath and keep the muscles in your face tense for a silent count of three or so. When you exhale, let all the muscles relax.

On your next deep inhalation, stretch your neck forward a bit and tense your shoulders. Hold the breath and the tightened muscles, then exhale, relaxing your neck and shoulders.

Repeat this general breathing and tensing, holding, and releasing process as you tighten each of the following areas in turn: upper chest, abdomen (this takes a little practice to do while breathing), buttocks, thighs, calves, and arch of foot and toes.

Finally, take a deep breath for a silent three count, hold it for the same amount of time, and exhale, also mentally counting to three. Repeat this cycle two more times, enjoying the feeling of how deeply relaxed you now are.

When you've deeply relaxed your body, it's time to test just how serene your mind is capable of becoming on its own. Keep your eyes closed and focus on the darkness behind your eyelids. Try to accomplish the state that mystics throughout the ages have referred to by various names, including "no mind" (a funny name for a mental state if you think about it). Basically, this is when no thoughts intrude on your inner peace. I prefer to call this mental state the *inner quiet*. Success at it to some level is a prerequisite for true mastery of mental powers and magick.

Quieting the Mind

Sit in your relaxed state and just observe the thoughts that enter your mind. As you'll be aiming for inner peace, the first thought you have will likely be: "What am I thinking about?" The next is just as obvious: "Have I quieted my mind yet?"

Let these and other disturbing thoughts come and go, but don't seek to banish them. Setting out to banish such mental intrusions is setting yourself up for failure. Merely observe the thoughts that pass and let them drift by on their own, as if the darkness behind your eyelids is an inky river capable of carrying them off.

Each time you attempt such mind calming, after each deep relaxation, you should find that less distractions enter your conscious awareness. How long should you practice? Let the amount of time you can go without becoming too distracted or, worse, falling asleep, determine how long. However, try to extend this period on a regular basis. After one short week of at least daily practice, the technique should result in your being able to remain in a reasonably quiet inner state for almost a minute. That's a pretty powerful state to achieve for the purposes of the rites you'll be using from this book.

But remember to merely let this happen. Don't force it or, again, you'll end up only asking your mind if it's succeeded yet. And each time it answers, it means you haven't succeeded yet!

Shortcuts to the Unseen

The inner quiet directly affects your psychic development. That is, as you get better at calming your mind, your abilities at visualization and concentration (which will become crucial later on) get better. And, consequently, as your abilities at visualization and concentration get better, your effort to quickly achieve the inner quiet becomes almost minimal. Your mind learns to quickly accept the quiet state as it learns to make the most of it.

All this mention of the importance of visualization and concentration shouldn't get you worried. Unlike other psychic training routines, the one you'll be following in this book is much more subtle, effective, and natural, if I do say so myself. But I'll let you be the judge, as you come to discover that you'll be learning by doing some pretty impressive and useful things.

The first of these "things" is autosuggestion. How's this for a short-cut to awakening some of your mystical faculties? You're about to, in a way, hypnotize yourself into contacting the unused parts of your mind!

Applying energy to thought is one of the secrets to making magick work. The rule also applies to autosuggestion (and suggestion, as we'll see later in the book), if in a slightly different way. With the rite given later in this section, you'll be able to both enter a deeper mind state, and forcefully accelerate the development of those mental tools you'll be calling on repeatedly.

You've already raised some energy during your circle castings (if you've started doing them). Here's a quick trick that will eventually improve your ability to do circles and help you raise emotion-driven energy that you'll need to draw on for all types of magick.

Quick Energy Raising

Think for a moment about something you like doing, or instead remember a decently fond memory. Sense how your body responds to this positive stimulus, either as a tingling or a calming sensation.

Now think about what you'd consider your favorite thing, or person, or pastime, or cherished memory. See how your body responds even more to this mental stimulus.

Then quickly switch to an unpleasant thought, shutting down for an instant the feelings you were generating. But before you have a chance to wallow in how empty your body feels. . . .

Immediately recall that best thought! Go with whatever increase in physical excitement that you feel as a result. Tense your muscles slightly to help build the sensation.

With time and repetition, you'll be able to summon such energy instantly, without relying on the associated memories.

Note that you should practice the preceding technique as often as possible, but not within the context of your other training. While you're still dependent on dredging up strong memories to achieve the energy raising, you'll find the process makes it hard to achieve a no-mind state. Instead of mixing the quick energy-raising with your other training, try doing it at idle moments, such as when waiting for a traffic light to change color or for a train to arrive at a platform.

After you've conditioned yourself to generate this energy instantly without the memory links, you can move on to applying this on-demand energy to autosuggestion and the awakening of your powers. To accomplish this end of power stimulation, you can use the following autosuggestion, which is hinged on your innate abilities to imagine the colors that make up white light, while sinking deeper into relaxation. It's a shortcut to power whose principles have been widely used in occultism, although never in this way.

Autosuggestion for Mystical Power

Perform a banishing and the relaxation routine, then do your best to achieve inner quiet.

With your eyes closed, look to the upper left of your inner dark field. It's okay to lift your head up in that direction a bit, to add to the feeling that you're trying to physically see toward the upper left.

Take a deep breath, and tense to raise emotional energy (but don't think of any memories to do so).

As you exhale, release the tensed energy and visualize in the upper left, with your eyes closed, a flash of red light. Don't worry if the color is not vibrant, only know it's there, and know it's there because you sent out energy to make it be there.

Continuing to breathe with the same deep rhythm, use your next inhaling and exhaling cycle to move your inner vision down and to the right a bit. That is, breathe in while moving your inner gaze, and exhale while fixing the new spot in your mind. To gauge how far down the move should be, consider that you will be moving to a total of seven such positions, ending at the lower right corner of your inner field of vision. The correct distance to move will become automatic after a few times doing this autosuggestion.

On your next inhalation, tense and raise energy. Exhale, releasing the energy and visualizing a flash of orange. Again, just know that it's happening if you don't see it clearly.

Move down and to the right on your next breathing cycle.

Repeat the charged visualization with a yellow flash. Then go on to alternately move diagonally down and raise energy to see each of the other rainbow colors you know are coming: green, then blue, indigo, and violet. (About indigo, though . . . it's between blue and violet in hue, but no two of us will ever see it the same way. Just do your best to see this quite indefinable color of the light spectrum.)

After seeing violet, continue to breathe deeply for three cycles.

Then take one extra-deep breath, tensing stronger than you did for each of the colors in the cycle. Raise up a blast of energy as startling as you can, and say a mantra, out loud, that you want to plant in your subconscious to make a reality. This is the most powerful part of the suggestion, and the one with limitless possibilities. For now, exhale and say something like:

The unseen world is readily open to me. My inner sight is true and far reaching.

Now, as disjointing as it may feel, count to three out loud and open your eyes. Do not think of what you just did—immediately try to get involved in another activity.

The previous autosuggestion should be done as often as possible, in darkness, even if you can't do a banishing first. The colors will become more vibrant, the impact on your ability to achieve inner quiet quite noticeable. Trust me at least on this, until you see for yourself the effects the autosuggestion will have on you.

Now, some other uses for this rite.

Suggesting Change in Your Life

Nocturnal Witchcraft, like many other mystical paths, is theurgic in nature. This means that its practitioners should consider self-improvement one of the most important goals. Granted, we should try to become masters of our mental and magickal powers, but theurgy also means striving to eliminate as many everyday or "mundane" flaws as possible.

From time to time, consider some of the things that hold you back from having the best relationship possible with the God and Goddess. To master divine powers, we must become more like Divinity, in other words.

Do you have a quick temper or, to the opposite extreme, an inability to care much about others? Maybe you find you're too active and unfocused, or perhaps too lazy? Are you often obsessive about others or particular things, or do you have a fear of committing to anything you believe in? There are numerous such pairs of imbalanced nature to watch out for. Do you fall into one end of these extremes? You have to be honest with yourself in picking the things you feel hold you back from development.

The autosuggestion technique we just covered can be used to banish what you consider to be your personal flaws. It can even help you kick a particular bad habit or destructive addiction to . . . well, something not very good for you.

Once you identify something that's bringing you down, or even hurting you and those you love, you can create a positive suggestion to wipe it out. Perform the autosuggestion technique as normal, but instead of delivering the "unseen world" line to your subconscious, state the positive suggestion you wrote.

Just one thing to keep in mind here: Make your suggestion positive! Do not state what you are trying to stop, only mention how you'd like yourself to be, and do so in the present tense. In other words, repeat how you already are the way you wish to be. For example: "I am calm and consider my actions before reacting," or, "I am master of my time and always make best use of it."

And so on.

Autosuggestion can be a powerful way to apply your still developing ability of relaxing and finding the inner quiet. Use autosuggestion repeatedly, and watch the amazing results.

On to more uses of these new mental states you're mastering.

Visualizations You Can Mold

Like autosuggestion, the skrying techniques in the following chapter will also contribute to rapidly accelerating your visualization and concentration capabilities. But it doesn't hurt to start giving yourself some additional boosts in the development of this ability.

If you have a tarot deck you're comfortable with, you're ready to begin the following. Otherwise, pick up one that speaks to you. Finding the right deck is easier than ever, as a lot of stores now have sample decks you can look through. If possible, use a deck that has illustrated pips (the cards in the four suits—one of pentacles, two of swords, and so on). I've become a fan of *The Secret Tarots* deck, by Marco Nizzoli. It's a dark one you might want to check out.

For now, in these pages, we won't be using a deck for divination. Although you're, of course, free to experiment with tarot divination, the deck you buy will, for the purposes of this book, be used for a form of skrying. And this is a form of skrying you should get started on as soon as you can. Even before you read the next chapter on skrying!

What follow are a couple of ways to play with the claylike nature of visualizations. The only things you need are your cards (for the first technique), candlelight, and a chair positioned in front of either your altar or some kind of table.

Animated Tarot
Perform at least a banishing and try to achieve some inner quiet.

Look at the faces on the cards, and pass the cards from one hand to the other. Let the images pass before you until one stands out. Even if you're familiar with the deck, one will catch your eye. The cards in a well-done deck represent a complete range of universal energies, and the focus of at least one card will match your mood on any particular night. Go with your instinct here, but try not to make it the same card every time.

Take the card that stands out to you and place it face up on your altar. If the card is glossy, position it so that the candlelight isn't causing a glare on the surface.

Let your gaze fall on the aspect of the card that captured your attention. Is it the flag that Death carries? The reflection in the water of the Moon? Whatever it is, try to focus on that spot.

Take a deep breath and blur your vision slightly, without taking your eyes off the now blurry part of the card. Wait for a silent three count, then exhale as you refocus or clarify your vision on the symbol. Again, wait for a silent three count, lungs empty, and continue to look at the image clearly.

Perform the previous step two more times.

Now, take a deep breath, blur your vision, do a three count, and exhale. Do not let your vision clear this time, however! Keep breathing deeply while gazing at the symbol out of focus. Your eyes should start to feel very uncomfortable.

When it feels like your eyes want to give in and close, let them do so . . . slowly. Allow your lids to slide shut so slowly, in fact, that in the near dark of candlelight you won't even be sure if you really did shut your eyes. You'll see what I mean by this. Your eyes might, for instance, stay open a crack, close, reopen a bit, then close again for a few seconds.

While your eyes are fluctuating between open and closed states, silently assert to yourself that you can still see the blurry symbol on the card. When they're really half open, your eyes will reveal it to you. When your eyelids are shut, however, what you see might shock you. Through the tiniest crack, the candlelight will help you "see" the blurry illuminated image. Achieving this state where you're uncertain whether your eyes are open or closed takes some practice, but it does help trick your mind into filling in the blanks of what is a forming visualization.

When you feel that you might be seeing the blurry image with your mind's eye, test it by forcefully shutting your eyes and trying to see the blur. Some of the image may have imprinted on your retina—almost as if you had looked at a glowing light bulb then shut your eyes. Imprinting is fine, as it will give your mind some light to mold. But if you can't see the blurry image at all, try the previous step's fluctuating eyelid stages for a minute or two longer and see what happens when you try forcefully shutting your eyes again.

In time, you should end up with some combination of a visualized and "imprinted" blurry image. When you're sure you're seeing something with your eyes closed, proceed to. . . .

Take a deep breath. Hold it in for a three count, also holding the blurry image in your mind's eye. You're going to now tap into the subconscious rhythm you set up a few minutes earlier. Exhale, trying to refocus your inner vision and clarify the blurry image. Keep your lungs empty for another three count as you continue to imagine that the symbol before you is clear.

Chances are you won't succeed fully the first time. Don't worry. Keeping your eyes closed, repeat the previous step, letting the visualized image go blurry on your inhalation. Perhaps your next exhalation will result in a clearer image. I recommend cycling between blurry and clear at least three times. You should find that each exhalation does result in a clearer image.

On your fourth deep breath, try to keep the image clear. If it won't quite stay put, perform more blurry-to-clear cycles.

Once you can hold the object clear in your mind's eye, breath in, hold your breath for a three count, and exhale, trying to see some movement of the object. A ripple in a flag or pool of water, a movement of the creature—whatever seems logical for the image you chose.

Repeat the previous step at least two more times, letting the image move on your exhalations.

Developing visualization skills is a lot easier when you know some tricks or secrets, if you will. The previous technique takes advantage of two little-known ones.

The first is that it's not necessary to see a form clearly to work with it. In the animated tarot technique, we worked with this idea in a literal fashion, bending an image from blurry to clear and back. But this principle also holds in any mystical working when you're having a hard time visualizing and making out anything at all. If you get only the sense that your desired image is there, somewhere, in the dark of your inner vision, then go with it. Try to animate or otherwise use that indistinct form. It may not get clearer, but the form you set out to imagine next time might.

The second secret to keep in mind is that moving or changing a visualization in some fashion helps it solidify in your mind's eye. The real or physical world is in constant motion, after all, so it makes sense that you can give your mental constructs added depth or reality by animating them.

After you have a little success at animating the tarot, you might want to try this next, more advanced technique. You won't need the cards, but should still have a chair set up in plain view of a candle. Just do not try this technique right after doing the tarot one. Make certain at least a few hours separate the two sessions, as this following technique requires that your eyes and concentration be unstrained and fully relaxed.

Also, set aside at least a half hour to do the exercise. Afterward, you may be really glad you did, as you'll see.

Phantom Lights

Perform a banishing and spend a few moments achieving some degree of inner quiet.

Gaze at the candle flame for a few moments. Without consciously doing so, find the "right" way to look at a flame of this intensity. Let your eyes adjust, refocus, subtly squint, or whatever. This should only take about minute.

Now comes the easiest work on developing your powers that you'll ever do. For the next thirty minutes or so (you can use a timer if you'd like) you'll basically just sit there! Don't worry, though—you will have something to look forward to. For as long as possible (maybe twenty-eight of the next thirty minutes you plan on sitting), resist the temptation to close your eyes. Do give in to the visually strange things your eyes will begin to experience, however.

After a while, maybe halfway through the session, you'll find it difficult to keep your eyes open. This will be when the first illusory phenomena begin to manifest. As you squint, fighting to keep the candle in view (and, perhaps, fighting to stay awake), the flame will begin to be surrounded by something quite odd: moving lights or bits of phantom glare. I call it the corona effect. You'll know it when you see it.

As soon as you become aware of the corona, begin adjusting your vision to increase the intensity of the phantom glare. This will take some almost subconscious altering of how much you're squinting as well as how much you're letting your vision go blurry. It might not be easy the first time, but you should be able to, with a couple of sittings, really get the corona glowing bright and "dancing" for you.

After the frequency and intensity of the glowing lights increase, experiment with seeing the phenomena farther away from the flame. Never let the flame leave your field of vision, but do let your gaze drift slightly to the right and left and up and down. Try focusing from time to time on any bits of corona that seem particularly bright or interesting. Most of these will flit away or disappear altogether when you scrutinize them—keep scanning and refocusing your attention. Eventually, you'll enter a state where you find that the brighter corona effects don't vanish. This might not come about on your first sitting. If nothing appears after the half-hour period, stop and try again another time. Making the attempt for longer than a half hour will result in a counterproductive strain on your vision.

But what if the corona does manifest? When you finally find that you can focus on a bit of glare without it disappearing, stick with it. Play around again with blurring your vision and squinting. The corona fragment should change with the different ways of looking at it that you attempt. It may grow in brightness or size or both. It may sharpen into a tiny, dense sphere. For a minute or two, let it do what it will.

Next you will try to modify the corona fragment. Still barely keeping your eyes open, perform similar deep breathing as you did when animating the tarot card. Breathe in, letting your eyesight blur on the corona. Hold for a silent three count, maintaining your blurry view. When you exhale, play with your vision to achieve a clear or sharp view of the phantom light. Hold your lungs empty for a three count, trying to hang on to the clear view.

Perform the deep breathing cycle two more times. After you do so, your eyes will be even more ready to close. No need to fight it at this point.

As you did with the tarot method, let your lids slide shut almost imperceptibly. Again, for the few seconds it's happening, your changing eyelid state should be a mystery. You shouldn't be too clear as to whether your eyes are open or shut. Be sure of only one thing: Maintain a view of the glare! If the glare starts to disappear, force your eyes open a little to recapture its view.

What happens next is very much up to you. The experience can go one of two ways.

For one, the corona might expand, filling your entire view and presenting a genuine vision! There's not much more I can say about this possibility except that you should let it happen. You might see a scene or a symbol that you have to interpret, but what you see will be worth the distraction from visualization training. And, seeing such a thing will only reinforce what a powerful visualization should look like. (More on visions in the next chapter.)

Barring the appearance of a vision, you will be trying to keep the corona visible to you after you close your eyes, just as you did with the tarot image. Perform three deep breathing cycles, blurring then clarifying the image in your mind's eye, again, as you did with the tarot symbol.

After the third time you clarify the glare in your mind's eye, you can begin having some fun with it. Relaxed as you are, begin to mold the glare to resemble any simple object that comes to mind. Experimenting with modifying the shape and color will have a major impact on your visualization abilities. When deciding what to make the light look like, pick something you can remember the details of, so you'll know right away if you're really seeing what you wish to see.

Continue to experiment with modifying the image for as long as you like, or as long as you can keep from feeling threatened by sleep. You decide when to finish; however, leave your eyes closed for this last step during your first couple of sittings.

After you've gotten proficient at your modifications of the candle glare, practice tilting your body to the left or right, then opening your eyes. With the candle now to your right or left, you'll be presented with a reasonably dark view of the room. Can you still see your image against this open-eyed blackness? Being able to do so is something worth striving for.

It seems important to point out one last time that the preceding visualization techniques will jumpstart dramatically your ability to see the unseen. However, they are only the beginning. While you should repeat them as often as you can, you'll also find it beneficial to make use of your burgeoning powers with simpler exercises. The kind of simple techniques you may have read about in the past will help.

For instance, if ever you have nothing to do in the darkness, exercise your mind's eye. Try to see, with eyes closed then open, increasingly complicated objects. But then, take what you learned in this chapter and apply it. That is, animate the images you see. Modify them. The groundwork you'll be establishing by doing so will come in useful for most everything you set out to accomplish in part three of this book.

Now, on to another way of seeing fantastic images against a dark backdrop of sorts.

Chapter Six

Divining by Night

Psychic quiet time.

This classification of night's late hours is worth repeating, perhaps under your breath, from time to time. Have you yet to listen during the hours of 3 to 5 A.M. with this in mind? Have you witnessed for yourself how these hours are free from excessive mental activity or psychic influence? If you haven't tried to detect the difference in the air when most people are asleep in your vicinity, make sure you do so tonight.

Better yet, make tonight the first time you begin using these mystical hours to your benefit.

We'll be exploring some simple ways to boost your basic powers of receptivity during psychic quiet time. However, these are not purely passive skills you'll be developing. They will allow you to receive inspiration from the dark deities, and to solve complex problems. These powers you'll soon master will also be put to further use when you begin to work with the skrying techniques taught later in this chapter.

Letting in the Signals

Like many techniques in Witchcraft, the one you're about to work with is based on sympathetic principles—on the occult concept of like attracts like. What, therefore, is the best way to sympathetically work with the psychic lull or quiet time? You've already learned it: the inner quiet. Now you'll learn how to take it a step further.

Continue to work on letting yourself link with night's "consciousness." That is, continue to practice deep relaxation and the passive removal of distracting thoughts, as these will open the way for the impressions of darkness to seep in.

Now, the night doesn't think, of course, but it does embody all things dark. Should you desire to let any energy of this type into your life, be it inspirational or tangible, you can let it in through your link to the night. From bits of advice offered by night's deities to information gleaned by psychic reconnaissance, benefits abound for the Nocturnal Witch who listens to the night in the special way shown here.

First, know that merely making your mind blank might not be enough to ensure your initial encounter with dark inspiration. For the first couple of times you attempt to access the unseen, you will need to focus on perfecting the sensory deprivation part of the following technique, to make certain that your normal, waking consciousness offers minimal interference.

To perform the technique, you will need a bed or the chair you use for doing the deep relaxation. You will actually be doing the deep relaxation first, then staying in place afterward, so keep this in mind when selecting a spot. The piece of furniture should be located in a quiet room. In all likelihood, any room is pretty quiet at about three in the morning, but do your best to minimize even the sounds of heat or air-conditioning or a humming refrigerator.

Find the darkest, most quiet room, but also make sure it doesn't feel either cold or warm. True room temperature (around sixty-seven degrees) is what you're going for. Your body shouldn't feel or sense the room—this includes drafts. No room may be perfect for this rite without at least some modifications, such as insulating a window or adjusting the thermostat. Consider this and act accordingly before proceeding.

You'll also need a simple blindfold—a folded cloth will do. A ball of cotton ripped in half will make two affordable earplugs.

Set up a simple altar or a table in front of you. If you're in bed, have some kind of table next to you. The only thing that really needs to be on this table is a lit candle, the blindfold, and earplugs.

Have an idea about what you wish to accomplish. Again, the first few times you try the following technique, you will need to concentrate on getting it right and making it work. But after that, you will want to use the technique most times to receive the dark inspiration we discussed. In such cases, form a concrete idea about what you need help with before you prepare your working area.

The candle should be the only light in the room for a few minutes before you're ready to proceed.

Listening to the Night

Perform the banishing.

Look up into the subtle darkness and say:

Lord and Lady of Night, be with me during this quiet time. Unseen ones, let your whispers break through the silence. Reveal to me (state your need; for example, "how I can remove this harmful influence").

Insert your earplugs.

If you have glasses, take them off. Grasp the blindfold in a way that will allow you to tie it on easily. Blow out the candle, and let your open eyes begin to relax in the darkness.

When the orange imprint or afterglow of the candle flame vanishes, shut your eyes. Tie on the blindfold.

Carefully sit back or lie down and begin to get comfortable.

Perform the deep relaxation.

Begin to achieve some inner quiet, letting thoughts come and go. However, you should interrupt this process after a minute or so with the following step.

Think, actively, about how quiet it is, about how black your surroundings are. Spend a few minutes achieving not exactly an inner quiet, but something more like an emulation of the *outer* quiet. Fill your mind with the awareness of the void surrounding you. Think of nothing else until this concept of void seems all too real, or for as long as you can do so without your attention wandering.

Then think of nothing at all, emulating the outer void within you, perhaps for a few seconds.

For the next minute or two, go back and forth achieving awareness of the void around and within you. This dual awareness of nothing will take some practice (and don't most mental exercises contain one or more steps requiring practice?).

Something strange will begin to happen. You will feel an overwhelming sensation that you are weightless—more etheric than material. Go with this. Don't let it jar you out of your relaxed, tuned state.

Now, wait. Let the impressions come. If you made a particular request, you may be shocked to find that clear answers or ideas about your query are appearing. They may come as images, they may be nothing more than thoughts, but they will seem alien to the way you've thought about said problem in the past.

The preceding technique can also be done "on the fly," so to speak. If you ever wake up during the hours of 3 to 5 A.M. (approximately), it may be night's way of trying to reveal something to you. Close your eyes and try to initiate the process from that point where you'd normally begin thinking about how quiet it is around you (chances are it will be dark and quiet enough to do so).

The final structure that this book should take on came to me in just such spontaneous sessions.

You don't have to wait for inspiration to take advantage of your relaxed state when coming out of sleep. You can also set an alarm to wake you, and then jump right into that step where you contemplate the silence around you. Of course, if you do set an alarm, you should have decided the night before on something to ask about. Don't waste your initial waking time, when you're still relaxed, trying to come up with something. You'll only jar yourself into less relaxed consciousness.

On Dreams

Night will not always wake you to impart its wisdom.

During psychic quiet time, inspiration may quietly seep into your subconscious and begin to take form, most often in symbols you find meaningful. Then, when these thoughts have taken on their own reality in your mind, you will be allowed to see them . . . at a time when you're likely to wake up when one of these mind-movies is in process. Let's face it, as rough as it is, most of us have to wake shortly after psychic quiet time on at least some of the days of a week. Our subconscious knows this. Sometimes we'll wake within the hours of five to seven even if we don't need to, having just experienced a particularly vivid picture show.

We're speaking, of course, of dreams, and of those that night wants you to remember; that is, those dreams that wake you up—you just won't remember any others!

Everyone dreams. Some don't remember their dreams from time to time, a result of waking up between REM sleep cycles. But if you sleep longer than an hour or so, you'll dream. If you wake up even at the tail end of a dream, you'll remember what you saw (with a little practice you'll be able to do so in entirety).

Most times, these dreams will be your subconscious remembering highlights of your day, getting some exercise, letting off some steam, or working through anxieties. We won't go into such mundane dreams here. If you're interested in why you keep finding yourself about to take a test in class while wearing only your underwear, check out a book on the non-occult nature of dreams from your local library.

We're concerned here only with the dreams that fit two criteria: those that occur somewhere near the end of psychic quiet time or up to about two hours after, and those that make you think there's something about them you just can't dismiss. The first requirement is pretty straight-forward, so on to the one that's not so obvious.

Ever since getting into the occult back in the 1980s, it has amazed me how normal most of my dreams remained. Even after performing an evocation of a spirit or having a powerful visionary experience in a skrying tool, I could still have dreams about talking banana cream pies and staircases that went on for hundreds of steep feet with no end in sight. Okay, so maybe they weren't always normal! But still, there wouldn't be entities trying to break through every time I nodded off.

Yet every so often, a dream would materialize that did seem out of the ordinary. A dream that didn't focus on seemingly chaotic rehashes of my day, or contain obvious repetitive themes that were clearly my mind trying to deal with some anxiety. No, from time to time a dream with unmistakable symbolism would just happen.

Look in your own dreams for relevant symbols that are constant. Dreams are chaotic normally, and things and people in them change often (that neighbor on the corner whom you're asking for a ride suddenly turns into your cousin offering you a drink at a party, for instance). Dreams containing nocturnal, mystical inspiration, however, feature objects, people, and acts that not only mean something, but stick around long enough to make you take notice. Look for the obvious, such as an image from a tarot deck, an occult tool, a magickal act, or even some mysterious figure in the act of giving you advice. Look also for the images that are so odd they don't take on an obvious connotation. A sense that everything is a particular color or maybe related to a particular element (earth, air, fire, water) may make a dream worth analyzing. Also, a truly bizarre symbol that you don't even recognize is a clear sign that something outside your normal subconscious is at work.

Interpreting such occult-related dreams will be a personal affair. Ultimately, only you can discover what an image or theme means to you. Dream interpretation books tend to get a little silly sometimes, as they assume a particular image, such as a black cat, would mean the same thing to everybody. How different a superstitious person would see such a creature than would someone who has a cat as his or her familiar.

Symbols abound in the occult world. Gathering them in books is easy and has been done hundreds of times. Decoding them is not such a simple matter. Unfortunately, I've got no shortcuts to share in this respect. You can check encyclopedic guides if you wish to see if any stock attributions make sense, but don't expect to be so thrilled with what you find.

What I can offer is a technique for decoding symbols. In fact, I already revealed it to you in this chapter. If you're stuck on what a particular symbol might mean to you, make that symbol the focus or "question" when you listen to the night. What better way is there of deciphering something than going back to the source of the symbol? During such a session, you may see the symbol again, but in a different context. You may see the symbol animated, thereby revealing its function in your life at the current time. Or, you may be told, either in a thought or what sounds like a voice from the shadows, what the symbol means to you.

You won't always need to resort to the full technique of listening to the night, however. Your abilities at knowing at a glance what a symbol means will increase with continuing practice and development of the important skill discussed next.

Gazing into Darkness

Working with the unseen energies of night is a recurring theme in our nocturnal tradition. Again, night is the ultimate physical manifestation of all things dark—the time when most of the powers and rites in this book will work best. And it is so much more.

It is tangible.

The darkness of night is something you can immerse yourself in. Almost fluid, nocturnal ether is what helps your magickal circle maintain its form, and is the very stuff you'll be molding to create miracles later on.

Night is also something you can look to when searching for visions and inspiration. In this chapter, you've already begun the process with sensory deprivation, letting some of the signals around you come in. Now you'll continue, learning how to actively peer into the blackness to see vibrant images and light.

The technique for mastering skrying that is revealed here can be done with either your nocturnal portal or a natural manifestation of darkness. We've covered the portal—now let's tarry for a moment, exploring the natural skrying option.

First, consider that you can't always have a nocturnal portal with you. If you travel a lot, you can buy something like a small obsidian egg (I use a five-inch one that offers an excellent skrying "window"). But even if you do have a portable device, you won't always have it with you. What do you do in such cases?

Second—and perhaps more important—there may come times when you want to connect with the night in its purest form. Outdoor Witchcraft rituals are powerful; outdoor nocturnal ones are hauntingly so. When you're outdoors, is it best to focus your attention on a bit of glass or stone?

For one of these reasons, there will be times when you want to try skrying the night itself. It's always charged, always dedicated to the service of . . . itself! The night is ready to help a skryer walking a dark path, much as a sacred grove would help one following a Druidic tradition.

Except you can find the night everywhere.

Now, I don't recommend just looking up at a clear night sky and skrying. Even on the night of a Dark Moon, stars will distract you. After a while of "stargazing," you'd end up experiencing an effect like that provided by the candle flame in the last chapter's visualization training. You can try using them for visualization practice, but star fields in clear night skies are not suitable for skrying.

On certain occasions, you may use an overcast night sky, but only if your surroundings (for miles) are dark enough to prevent a glowing illumination of the clouds. That is, you won't find staring at a beige, gray, or perhaps orange sky very helpful. Natural lighting is not the only thing to watch out for. Depending on how thick the clouds are, you might not be able to skry them unless the moon is set, or is Dark, or is a couple of days from having been or being Dark.

The most reliable way to skry the night, however, is to work with its effects on your surroundings. Even major cities will provide natural patches of darkness.

Best is a part of a natural body of water, ranging from stream to ocean, where no light is reflected. In New Orleans, with the gaslights of the French Quarter to my back, I skryed the Mississippi; at the opposite end of the lighting spectrum, I've used the technique closer to home, on Manhattan's East River (although parts of the Quarter are much quieter!). Again, make sure the patch of water contains no reflected light.

Shutting off all the lights in a room and looking out a window can work, if at least part of your view is of the shadows. This creates a natural kind of magick mirror or nocturnal portal. I did this facing just the right direction from a hotel room in Philadelphia.

Speaking of mirrors, the ordinary reflective mirrors you use to check your appearance can be used outdoors, too. Just position it at an angle where you can see only darkness and not yourself. You can even stare at the reflection of a clear night sky (but not a reflection of the moon), as the stars in most parts of the sky will not show up.

A natural hole in the ground observed on a starlit night can provide adequate depth to lose your gaze within. This is one I've used in several less-populated settings, ranging from Salem, Massachusetts, to Ormond Beach, Florida. I imagine the same would work for a cave, as long as you're sure there's nothing in it before you stare at its opening for a period of time!

I hope it's clear that no matter where you are or where you go, night impacts your surroundings in a way you can skry. Take advantage of this. Even a shadowy corner can work. Just make sure that light is either to your side or far enough behind you that it doesn't distract you.

Whether you use a natural portal or the one on your altar, skrying in the fashion we're about to explore can provide startling results—from finding answers to life's problems to getting crisp and vivid visions (even warnings) of things occurring elsewhere. That such amazing things can be accomplished either with the night or your portal shows how excellent a link to darkness the latter is, and why you should always have it on your altar.

Mastering the View

To make skrying work, you have to allow your psychic or astral senses to awaken. Doing so requires you to first somehow tune out your ordinary senses. Gazing into a tool or natural dark spot helps to accomplish this, acting as a form of sensory deprivation. Achieving inner quiet before such gazing only helps to increase the effect. The required altered state for skrying will happen naturally when you gaze after entering deep relaxation.

The altered state will also eventually help your other mystical senses develop. In time, you'll be able to hear sounds syncing up to the image in your skrying tool.

For now, though, back to how to prepare for the act.

As you may have gathered, success at skrying demands dim lighting bordering on total darkness. Any light present should not be visible as a reflection in your chosen tool. Outdoors, this means positioning yourself so that any light sources are either behind or to the side of you. Indoors, it means positioning a candle or two so that their soft light is similarly neither reflected in your portal nor within your peripheral field of vision.

Any lights affecting your working area should make the focal point stand out against the darkness and keep from calling attention to themselves. The ultimate goal, whether your focal point is natural or an altar-top portal, is to be staring into a blank field of darkness that's slightly lighter than the black night around you.

And this just-right view should be arranged with respect to your seated line of sight. You don't want to skry standing, so sit down to get the viewing angle and lighting just right. Where to sit? Outdoors, a rock or tree stump will do, as will sitting cross-legged if you're comfortable doing so. Indoors, use the same chair and table or altar setup as with the visualization exercises.

It is not necessary to work with full altar tools in place. Some find it easier to enter an altered state if they burn a little incense.

Having helped a lot people develop their inner vision and answered a lot of letters troubleshooting the initial steps of the process, I've come up with the following technique that is likely to get you an initial skrying vision faster than any other I've seen published. But again, don't take my word for it. Just do the following, omitting not a single step.

Perform a banishing and self-relaxation.

Achieve some inner quiet and perform the autosuggestion exactly as it is printed in chapter 5. After delivering the lines about the unseen world being readily open before you, however, do not count to three. Instead. . . .

Slowly open your eyes, letting your gaze fall on the skrying portal or focal point. Avoid focusing on the dark spot, though; let your gaze drift into it. Having performed the autosuggestion, you'll be more inclined to do this kind of passive viewing, anyway.

After you feel your gaze is being drawn into the tool, change nothing in your approach for a few minutes. Go with the experience. You might sense your vision becoming a little blurry, your eyes a little heavy. Do not close your eyes, however, as it will set you back, making you feel as if you need to do the autosuggestion again. Instead of closing your eyes, resist the urge, thereby letting yourself be lulled into a deeper state.

Maybe five minutes later, the apparent need to close your eyes will pass, being replaced by something both peculiar and wonderful. The dark field or portal will become lighter. I've often described this to others as resembling an old television tube that has suddenly sprung to life, yet which hasn't had time to form a picture. The field may seem to lighten in a more subtle way to you, however.

Now, before we continue, know that if the portal or field doesn't lighten after fifteen or twenty minutes of gazing, don't worry. It might be best to try again at another time. For many practitioners it does take a few sessions to coax the inner vision into springing forth and taking active control. Simply end your attempt after no more than twenty minutes of actual gazing to avoid unnecessary eyestrain and boredom.

But if the lightening does appear, remain calm and passive. Getting excited will snap you out of your altered state. The lighted look of the new field may persist for seconds or a minute before it starts to fade.

Replacing the subtle glow will be some type of simple vision. For most (according to my tallies of reader experiences), this will consist of a few phantom clouds moving all in the same direction. Personally, when my vision is opening during a session I instead see moving sparks of multicolored light that tend to range from drifting motions to chaotic bouncing. That is, I see the sparks if I don't go straight into a vision. And seeing a vision without preamble is another possibility. If you do see clouds or sparks or some other opening phenomena, however, know that these light shows will pass.

When the opening phenomena fade into more meaningful images, brace yourself. Here, your experience with visualization molding might prepare you for seeing a vision with your eyes open. Passively let the picture develop or even move before you. More often than not a vision will have some animation to it, even if it's just a still image moving around your skryed field—kind of like the image from a slide projector would move, if the latter were shifted with the power turned on.

Don't concern yourself too deeply with the nature of the image floating in the ether before you. Right now, you're still training your ability to activate your skrying faculties at will. However, should the

image stir something within you, or seem to have some occult significance (as discussed in our dream discussion earlier), contemplate its
possible meanings after the session ends.

While practicing, also try to listen for any sounds you might hear.
In time, an increasing number of your visions will begin to have ac-
companying audio components. These might start simply and faint, as
wispy as the sounds of wind or a faraway ocean. Don't actively seek out
sound for the first six or seven successes you have at skrying. Try to let
this aspect of your astral senses just come to you.

Follow the visions and possible noises for about five minutes. Go
longer if you can remain focused and have the time, but longer than
ten minutes will rarely yield new images, with the exception of a focused work, such as a communication with the dead (see chapter 13).

After a few weeks of regular practice, you should find yourself entering
the skrying state of mind with increasing ease and within a decreasing
amount of time. When you're confident that your abilities can be summoned with minimal effort, try attempting to skry with less initial
preparation. First omit the autosuggestion, then experiment with trying to get into the right state with only a quick relaxation and a minute
of inner quiet.

When you reach the point where skrying can be performed basically on call, you're ready to use it in a technique similar to the sensory-
deprivation one given earlier in this chapter. This listening to the night
while skrying will both boost your ability to hear the unheard and provide you with more tangible impressions from the dark. Of course, no
blindfold will be used, or no earplugs either, for that matter.

Don't use skrying in the following fashion just for fun, however.
Have some purpose or question when doing the following. You're
about to see and hear advice from the night and the Gods of Old.

The technique can be done with the inclusion of a nocturnal circle
casting or only a banishing (your choice). If you cast the circle, you'll

need your altar, fully set up, and a chair. Otherwise, the seated skrying configuration you've been using will be fine.

Perform the banishing. If you wish to also cast a nocturnal circle, do so up to step twenty-four (which ends with you skrying, anyway), and be sure to use your new abilities at the relevant points (peering into the invoking pentagrams, and so on).

Let your skrying fully awaken in your chosen focal point. Say:

Lord and Lady of Night, be with me during this quiet time.
Unseen ones, let your whispers break through the silence.
Unseen ones, show me the way through my current plight.
Reveal to me (state your need).

Maintain inner quiet as you skry, also allowing yourself to sink into the silence around you. Just as your skrying awakens more quickly with practice, so will the sense that you developed during your sensory deprivation experiments: the sense that you are emulating the outer quiet within. Fill your mind again with the awareness of the void surrounding you.

Experiment for a minute or two achieving awareness of both the void around and within you. This dual awareness of nothing will help both your skrying and astral hearing fully activate.

The feeling that you are almost weightless will manifest, allowing you to go even deeper into your skrying focal point.

Let the visual and audible impressions come. In this deep state you should not only receive symbols, but a clear understanding of what they mean. You may even see a complete scene, with sound. It may show you handling a particular problem. It may show you the future or even the past if it led to your current concern. In any case, your visions should be unlike those you've ever seen.

After you get the sense that no further useful information will be forthcoming, thank the Gods in your own words for their inspiration.

If you performed a circle casting, proceed to perform the closing of it (from step twenty-eight on; there's no need for further invocation). Another banishing is a good idea if you didn't cast a circle. Either way, do partake in a simple cake and drink grounding when you're finished.

Begin to use skrying in your magickal workings on a regular basis. Apply it to all circle castings—there will be plenty of moments when you may catch a glimpse of the unseen. Apply it whenever the beauty of the moon's reflection on a body of water inspires you to seek insight from the Goddess.

Seeing imagery in the dark ether is a powerful part of Nocturnal Witchcraft. Use this developing skill whenever possible.

Chapter Seven

Mind Reading by Touch

This chapter and the one following it are ones you never thought you'd find in a book on Witchcraft, right? And I didn't even have to read your mind to know your opinion on the matter.

While not a practice associated with the traditional Craft, mind reading has its place in our dark current. More so, it depends on the nature of night for success. No doubt you've been getting the impression that the silence of night allows for the transmission of thoughts and other mental energies. Here's your chance to see just how far you can reach into the tangible medium of darkness, to see how easily you can pick thoughts out of the inky blackness around you.

Now, if your only exposure to mind reading has come from fiction, you may be surprised to know that the feat is possible. It may not always be as flashy or flawless as it's been in, say, Anne Rice novels, but it does work. Given practice, the ability can work startlingly well.

Be wary of those who openly claim to have the power, though. They are more than likely mentalists, or stage magicians who simulate mystical powers. When done in good-natured fun, such as by the Amazing Kreskin or David Blaine, such pseudo mind reading is perfectly ethical entertainment. For its success, mentalism relies on misdirection and other mostly good-natured chicanery, as well as an audience's willingness to be amazed.

Those with even a tiny bit of true mind-reading capabilities, however, remain silent. They know, through their insight, that certain things are best kept secret. Witches who develop the ability, in particular, already understand what it means to keep certain parts of their lives private.

I was always fascinated by mind reading, which is part of the reason I began studying mentalism a few years ago. Knowing that mentalism was a form of stage magic, I knew that understanding its principles would help me spot fraudulent psychic claims. Being trained in its ways would ensure I didn't waste my time looking into obvious frauds. Stage magic is the science of pretending to perform miracles; Witchcraft and magick are the practices of making real miracles, after all. Avoiding scams and wastes of time seemed worth the learning time I'd put in.

But developing debunking talents was not the only reason I sought out mentalism; one, just one, of its practices seemed awfully familiar to my occult-oriented mind.

That's Incredible, Indeed

It all clicked for me at a pretty young age, when I saw Kreskin perform a murder mystery feat on the show *That's Incredible*. I was young, sure, but had already been experimenting with the simple art of dowsing, using both Y rods (forked tree branches) and a pendulum. Dowsing basically relies on amplifying subtle, ideomotor movements in your body to a degree that brings them to your attention. Our bodies are more in tune with our subconscious than you might think. We're just not aware of it. A Ouija board can tap this link, gathering knowledge from the recesses of your mind (or another's mind!); so, too, can a pendulum or dowsing rod gather psychic impulses manifesting as ideomotor tremors in your body. Much more on dowsing in the next chapter, but for now simply know that dowsing tools and Ouija boards work on very similar principles, both amplifying impulses that your conscious mind is too busy or unfocused to notice.

Back to Kreskin's performance. I would later learn that what he did was a modification of an old stunt—one documented from over a hundred years ago, but seemingly much older. The performance involved a technique known as contact mind reading. In the particular show I saw, the feat performed proceeds as follows:

The mentalist (Kreskin in this example) leaves a room and arranges for four members of the audience to be randomly selected. A fake murder weapon is left on the stage, and the first of the selected four acts as a "murderer," pretending to kill a "victim," the second person who came to the stage. Murderer and victim return to their seats. The third audience member selected picks up the weapon and returns to his or her seat, hiding the weapon somehow. The fourth, the witness, remains on stage.

The mentalist then returns to the stage and, wasting no time, asks everyone in the room to think of the scene that just occurred. He then has the witness take his wrist and commands him or her to think of the victim and keep that person in his or her mind. Amazingly, the mentalist walks off with purpose, dragging along the witness by the wrist contact. The mentalist's other hand is held out before him, and he doesn't seem to really be seeing where he's headed (in some variations, a blindfold is even used). He moves through the crowd almost as if a seeing-eye dog leads him, with the witness also in tow. In time, maybe as soon as thirty seconds, the mentalist comes to the victim and rests his outstretched hand on the "body's" shoulder.

Not reveling in the applause, the mentalist then commands the witness to think about the murder weapon. In a few short moments, he zeros in on this as well, leaving only the murderer. Finding him or her, too, is a simple task.

Interesting, huh? Having read my simple description of dowsing a few paragraphs earlier, does contact mind reading seem familiar to you, too?

My curiosity never left after seeing this performance. Years later I would run into a great mentalist, or "perceptionist," as he often calls himself. This man, Joel Bauer, helped me get started in deciphering the techniques used by performers world round. I read all the classics of the art, met with Joel at various shows to discuss my progress, and pursued other stage magic training available here in New York City. But the real revelation came when I ran into a description of contact mind reading in a book that was filled with stage trickery: *The 13 Steps to Mentalism*, by Corinda. While every "effect" in the book was accompanied with the inside knowledge on how to pull off a trick, contact mind reading or muscle reading contained nothing but encouragement on practicing to get it right.

There was no trick involved!

I was fascinated, to say the least, and spent more time finding further descriptions of this elusive practice than I did researching anything else associated with mentalism. While Corinda's book only contained four and a half pages on contact mind reading, I soon found booklets describing the practice. I uncovered tales of one of its greatest masters, Hellstrom (Alex Vogt), from the 1920s and 1930s. I found turn of the twentieth century works by L. W. de Laurence and other occultists going into the merits of contact mind reading.

As you'll see, it is a form of dowsing, and when mixed with some other occult techniques, its practice can be expanded to that of receiving thoughts from afar.

After a little practice, you'll see a whole new meaning to the phrase "open mind."

Making Contact

The description of Kreskin's murder mystery has at its core the most simple form of contact mind reading. The practitioner lets a person take his or her wrist and asks the person to keep in mind some object (or other person) in the room. Then, using subconscious, ideomotor responses in the *subject*, the mind reader is able to use the subject's hold on his or her wrist as a living dowsing rod and walk around the room to find the item being thought of. Unlike dowsing, where it only feels as if the rod or pendulum is being moved by an outside force, contact mind reading relies on true external movement, that of a living subject. Contact-free mind reading, which we'll get to in the next chapter, relies on several types of responses in the mind and body of the practitioner, more like traditional dowsing.

Yet mastering contact-free reading is just about impossible without first getting down the contact practice. As I'll point out in many books for years to come, all magickal or psychic ability is natural, but naturally blocked in our minds. We develop in childhood subtle censors that block psychic ability. The adults around us during childhood teach us how to focus on physical, tangible reality, often at the expense of our links to the unseen. To make anything mystical work for you, you have to first bring down some of these censors. The best two ways to do this? Practice at what you're trying to develop, and experience a little belief-system shock from time to time.

In *Summoning Spirits*, for example, I first teach how to evoke entities to the astral plane where they can be skryed, and only then recommend that the reader try evocations to the physical plane. In *Contact the Other Side*, I recommend trying to get the voices of the dead on tape before trying to hear and see the deceased with the mind alone.

Again, mystical practice combined with gradual shocks to the censors—these are universal occult keys to development, as you'll find.

Practicing contact mind reading will slowly attune your mind to the subconscious mechanics necessary for linking with the mind of another. At first you'll mainly be relying on subtle movements in your subjects, and will have simple successes such as finding a thought-of object or spot in a room. As your mind becomes gradually amazed at your ability, however, it will "allow" you greater successes and the use of much more intuition. For instance, contact reading will eventually let you not only find an item being thought of, but will also enable you to perform some action with it—an action the subject was thinking of all along. These types of successes will be signs that the censors are finally breaking down, allowing for the reading of thought "vibrations" that transcend the movements of the human physical form.

For your initial attempts at contact mind reading, it's important that you pick the right type of person to help you out. This shouldn't be someone antagonistic or closed-minded. Pick someone who you trust to be honest and helpful, and who you're sure would rather see you succeed than fail. Let this person know you're about to try a neat experiment, but don't let him or her know much more at first. Gauge the level of interest he or she shows as you proceed. If it seems beneficial, then keep that person on tap for further experiments. You might not have the luxury of too many volunteers at first, but as your abilities improve you'll have no trouble finding people who want to be amazed, particularly at parties. Do try to eventually work with as many people as you can.

Contact Experiment One

Enter a small- to medium-sized room with your subject. This should be a room with plenty of objects around the perimeter, as well as one with an uncluttered floor.

Tell the subject to think of something in the room and hold it in his or her mind. Do not try to follow the subject's gaze, however. While a stage magician would love such a visual cue, you'll only be cheating yourself with this kind of shortcut.

Repeat to the subject the command, reminding him or her to keep the chosen object in mind. As you say this, place the subject's right hand on your left wrist (if you're left handed, place the subject's left hand on your right wrist). Ask the subject to grasp your wrist firmly.

Say that you're now going to find the thought-of object with his or her help, and immediately walk in a straight line along the wall nearest you.

One of two things will happen: You'll either freely feel the person going with you, or you'll feel some resistance. If the latter, change your direction until you feel no hesitation.

Move with determination, but slow enough so that you can scan the air over each object. That is, you'll want to have your projecting hand hovering out in front of you, acting in a similar fashion to the tip of a dowsing rod. Your receiving hand (the one being held) will be drawing in thoughts, at first in the form of your subject's resistance or loosening up to your lead. One day soon, you'll be actively drawing in much more from the very air around you.

Keep moving around the room—it's okay to circle it more than once—avoiding your subject's gaze. You will begin to sense, almost unconsciously, that the subject has a distinct pattern of resistance variation. Particularly if you circle a second time, you'll notice that the subject seems to want you to stop in part of the room. Basically, he or she will resist when you're moving in the wrong direction, and let you go only in the right direction. But when you pass the spot containing the object, a fiercer resistance should manifest. Try to narrow down the region containing the object. That is, walk back and forth to be sure of approximately a four-foot area that the subject seems to be "holding you" within.

Stand in the center of the discovered area. Close your eyes and slowly begin to sweep your arm from side to side in front of you.

This is where your level of development will alter the experience. If it's one of the first couple of times you try contact mind reading, you'll only know that you're pointing at the object when you feel from the subject some kind of tightening or jerking motion on your wrist. In time, you'll also feel a distinct tingling within or seemingly external pulling of the hand you're using to scan the air! Pay close attention to this external sensation I call "the pull," as it will factor heavily in the techniques revealed in the next chapter.

For now, using the wrist reactions of your subject and possibly the pull of your projecting hand, find the spot in the air that you believe to be the right one. Repeat your sweep of the air to be sure this is the one, and open your eyes.

Let your projecting hand move forward and possibly down or up. There should be, once again, a *lessening* of resistance on your contact wrist if you're on the right track now. The subject will here be in a state of amazement. Your projecting hand should move to pick up only the object that produces this lessening of resistance. Let it eventually just move in on the object that feels "right." Even the first time you perform this experiment, you may feel a tingle or tugging on your scanning hand. In time, you *will* feel such a pull.

Pick up or touch the object and ask if it's the right one. (You already know the answer, though!)

Experiment One should be repeated as often as possible to help you hone the impressions you receive through both hands.

Again, your receiving hand will be drawing in thoughts. What will take some practice is sensing the difference between hesitation and excitement in your subject. Sometimes a tugging on your wrist will mean "stop," and sometimes it will mean "wow, you found it." Discerning the difference is what throws more than a few beginners off at first.

Your projecting hand will be acting as a tuned divining rod, sending out some of the signals you're getting from the subject. The idea here is that like attracts like. The right object will draw your projecting hand through a kind of magnetism.

Again, don't take any of my theories as law until you try them out for yourself.

In time, with steady success, you will find that your receiving hand (the one your subject is holding by the wrist) isn't even contributing to the process of contact mind reading. When this begins to happen somewhat regularly—when you feel you're being pulled more by your projecting hand, as if it really were a dowsing rod—proceed to the following experiment, preferably using the person with whom you worked with the most ease during Experiment One.

Contact Experiment Two

Set five or six very different objects in a straight line on a table. Without looking at your subject, ask him or her to think of one of these items and to keep it in mind.

Both of you should take seats before the line of objects. Position yourselves so that your subject will be able to hold the wrist of your receiving hand, and also so that you can move your projecting hand over the line of items.

Close your eyes and try your best to achieve some inner quiet. This may be the first time you try doing so in the presence of others, so it may be difficult to achieve the type of calm that you're used to. Just do your best.

Open your eyes and repeat to the subject the command you made —that he or she should keep the object in mind. Do not look at the subject's face, however.

With the subject still holding your wrist, begin to slowly sweep your projecting hand over the lined-up objects. The idea is, obviously, to find the one that your subject is keeping in mind. How you do so depends on how long you've been working with Experiment One. Recall that the idea in that experiment was to, over time, rely more on your projecting hand to give you the pull (like a dowsing rod), the subtle cue that you're heading in the right direction. In this second experiment, you may get a tightening up or jerking from your subject on your wrist if you pass the right object, but it's unlikely that a cue from the wrist will actually help you to stop at the right one in the first place.

Reach down and pick up the object your hand somehow dips toward. Feel for that same sensation you started to get in your projecting hand after repeated practice of Experiment One.

Success will feel incredible. This will be your first almost pure implementation of dowsing the contents of someone's mind with little or no ideomotor assistance. Do not become discouraged if you fail a couple of times. Did you try this experiment only after getting dowsing-like success with Experiment One? If you didn't, work on that experiment longer before trying Experiment Two again.

You should be master of and attuned to the pulling sensations possible in both hands before proceeding to the next experiment.

Contact Experiment Three

This is another walking procedure, using the same type of room described in Experiment One (it can be one you used for that purpose). Ask your subject to think of an object in the room. However, tell him or her to not think of it as a static object—rather, to think of it in motion or in use somehow.

Give him or her a moment to think about the possible uses of said object. Then rephrase your command by saying, "Imagine something you'd like me to do with this object, and keep this thought in your mind. Imagine me actually using the object."

Have the subject grab your wrist and begin the same room-sweeping method covered in Experiment One, using whatever combination of receiving- and projecting-hand impulses you feel comfortable with.

When you think you've zeroed in on the object, most likely relying more on your projecting hand at this point, begin to reach for it. However, before you actually touch the thing, repeat the exact command you gave a few moments ago ("Imagine something you'd like me . . .").

Now, clear your mind as best as you can in this nonrelaxed state, and touch the object. As soon as you make contact, try to let your hand move automatically. It may jerk to one direction, or it may grasp the item a certain way. Let such an initial impulse come to you. On rare occasions, you may just perform the action your subject was thinking of, feeling it move as if powered by that invisible tingle or pull described in Experiment One. If this happens during your first attempt, great—you're ready to try the experiment with another subject. If you feel only a slight impulse or even nothing, however, proceed as follows.

Slowly lift the object, feeling for tension or a pulling on your contact wrist. There should be a minor (*really* minor) jerk from the subject each time you begin to get closer to doing the right thing—the higher you raise that cup to your lips, the closer to your ear you bring that conch, the more you turn over the snow globe, and so on. Try to move in accordance with what your subject unconsciously wants this way, while also trying to maintain some mild degree of inner quiet.

Whether you perform the chosen action by slowly interpreting your subject's arm movements, by following your own projecting hand's impulses, or eventually through a flash of inspiration, consider the experiment a success. Whichever way it comes about, such a success will be training your deeper intuition.

Repeat Experiment Three with different people and over the course of several days, at least. Don't become discouraged if it takes a while to master, and especially don't get bogged down in trying to guess every few seconds what action the person was thinking of. Only focus on the arm motions. They'll guide you, yes, but will also help you blank your thoughts enough to let the thoughts of your subject slip in. Inspiration will not come to you if you're actively seeking it out. Maintain whatever inner quiet you can, and allow yourself to focus on the impulses in both hands. Let your mind pull in whatever extra information it can at this point.

The progression through the aforementioned three experiments is very much one of sympathetic magick. Your physical or contact mind reading ability slowly evokes your mental mind-reading ability. Why this is so will become clearer as you move on to the contact-free techniques taught in the next chapter. Only move on to contact-free reading after achieving success at the three contact ones, however. Save yourself the frustration and discouragement of rushing on to advanced work unprepared.

Chapter Eight

Reading Minds Through the Ether

We're about to venture into the ability of reading minds without making physical contact. In fact, although you won't begin by using it in this way, this technique can eventually be used to read someone's mind without his or her awareness that you're doing so.

Possible dangerous ground, karmically speaking!

So, before we get to the how-to, let's examine the when-to and when-not-to. It's now a good time to cover some important caveats, and get into the ethics of power.

Mind Your Own Business?

We're about to venture into techniques that can help you get information from people without their consent. Please tread carefully if you do choose to pry in such a fashion. This is one of those areas of magickal practice you likely haven't seen rationalized before. While the "evil" of doing something such as casting a love spell on an unsuspecting person has been discussed in dozens of books, the karmic consequences of taking information against another's will hasn't been so much as touched on in even a dozen words.

True, mind reading hasn't appeared in many modern occult texts; however, that's not the only reason you won't find much written about its ethics. Mind reading, like other "powers," spells, and rituals, is neutral—the way it is applied at any given moment is what can be classified as good or evil, not the practice. How can any author comment on what you do with mind reading or even magick for that matter? We can try, but in the end your application of a mystical ability will always be determined on a case-by-case basis. You will have to rely on your own sense of ethics. There's nothing inherently evil in a computer, for instance, but it can be used for everything from criminal hacking to tracking a hospital patient's progress. It is the user who determines what he or she will do with a tool, and who, ultimately, must take responsibility for these actions.

Before you try to read minds without someone's consent—that is, outside of an experimental setting—consider both why you want a particular piece of information and how you plan to use it. Certainly, a person who fears for his or her safety can do a scan to see if a shifty individual actually does intend harm. Also, there's nothing karmically wrong with finding out if someone's lying to you about something important—something that could have a negative impact on your life. Maybe someone knows something that he or she has no right withholding from you; maybe someone has a secret that could save you a lot of grief.

Now, you can't go around using mind reading to satisfy your paranoia. In fact, if you overuse the ability in this way, you will be subject to more than just bad karma and the chance of universal payback (threefold or not). Mentally calling everyone a liar and challenging them with your abilities will lead to some hard-to-overcome blocks in your subconscious. Put simply, you will associate mind reading with such a high level of stress that your subconscious will shut off, in self-defense, your access to these abilities.

How's that for a built-in system of ethical checks and balances?

Assuming you don't go on a mind-reading spree, you will be occasionally faced with the question of whether it's appropriate to use your ability. For such occasions when you're not sure about how to proceed, consider if you would want this type of mind reading done to you. I know that sounds a bit cliché, but the principle that is found in several religions, including Christianity, sums it up. "Do unto others . . ." really is the best way to judge whether you're crossing the line. By thinking of the possible universal consequences of mind reading and indeed all your mystical acts, you'll go far toward maintaining a positive balance in your karmic account.

Let's take a seemingly harmless, social application of mind reading as an example. We'll leave out the technical details of the mind dowsing technique mentioned, as the how-to will be covered in the next section.

You're at a club, having a drink. Scanning the crowd, you come across a person whom you find attractive. You want to meet this person, but are more than just shy. Maybe you're new to this hangout and don't want to tick off the wrong person or gain a negative reputation. Perhaps you're interested in someone of the same sex, and aren't sure how he or she would respond. And regardless of your orientation, perhaps the person you're approaching would just love an excuse to use you to aggravate a jealous lover who also happens to be lurking at the club.

For whatever the reason, you decide to play it safe. You decide to do a little mind probe.

Using an advanced form of mind dowsing, you pose some silent yes or no questions to the person, without his or her knowledge. Getting the answers you want, you lift your drink and make your way over to the fellow clubgoer.

Anything wrong with this? Let me ask this another way: How would you feel if you were on the other end of the probe?

What if you would possibly be interested in the person reading you, but felt that it was best not to get involved with anyone right now? Surely, the mind reader would distract you by approaching you under the assurance that you're an easy score.

What if you were intrigued, but in a relationship and didn't really want to be bothered? The mind reader might have only picked up that you would be interested, but not that you're currently unavailable.

What if the mind reader is not quite as good at the art as he or she believes to be the case? You wouldn't like being hounded by someone under false pretenses.

These are just a few examples of why you have to try to put yourself in your subject's place before exercising your power. Certain predicaments clearly make mind reading justifiable. For instance, if you thought your life was in danger and had to identify some bit of information critical to your escape, no one could question the ethics involved in getting such information through probing. But more often than not, you'll have to rely on your sense of right and wrong, and your honesty as to whether you'd be okay with the power being used on you.

Again, with mystical abilities, the cliché of doing unto others applies.

Oh, and one more important point: Try to set up some rigid guidelines for when you should never use your power. I, for example, never read the mind of a loved one or friend without consent (that is, outside of an experiment). This helps me maintain an ethical respect for the power and what it can do, and helps me maintain the trust of those whom I respect. Consider doing the same.

With that said, we can move on. You're about to learn how to pick up the thoughts of others when you're right in front of them. With a little practice, this contact-free mind dowsing will startle you with its accuracy, and will change how you interact with others forever.

Mind Dowsing Basics

Remember those "other" feelings you would get during contact mind reading? The pulling sensations you'd have in your projecting hand?

There's a reason I asked you to be sure you started feeling them before trying anything in this chapter.

With attunement to these feelings, the mind can be used as a powerful dowsing tool.

Rods, pendulums, and other seemingly automatic devices cannot work on their own. All such objects rely on your mind's ability to focus on the wavelength or subtle vibrations, if you will, of an object.

And with the conscious or unconscious help of another, the object you focus on can be a thought.

Most dowsing implements, such as rods or pendulums, work on a binary principle. That is, they answer your question or challenge with yes/no, left/right, up/down, proceed/don't proceed, or some other binary response. For example, when dowsing for water you're essentially asking the rod if there's water below you; if there isn't any you move on, waiting for a "yes" or dipping response.

But for dowsing to work you must know what you're looking for!

This idea is the basis for all the mind reading techniques taught in this book. After all, thousands of psychic impulses and energies surround us at any moment. While at night many of these signals subside, possibly down to the hundreds if someone could count such things, the number of possible things you can tap into is still enormous. You couldn't just reach out in most cases and hope to pick up some useful information from another. You need to pick what you're after so that you can do some binary dowsing of the information. For instance: Does he or she mean me harm? Is this the person who can help me accomplish my goal tonight?

You need to narrow the type of thought you're after as much as possible for mind reading to work. Get it down to the simplest question or statement that can be tested with binary dowsing (more in a moment on how to determine the yays or nays in such a process).

However, just knowing what you're looking for doesn't guarantee that the thought is in the mind of the other person right now.

The mind is a chaotic environment. You can't expect to etherically waltz into someone's mind and dig through mental files. It just doesn't work that way. In *Gothic Grimoire* you'll learn an advanced technique for listening to some random thoughts of others and picking up general intentions and impressions from them from far away. However, this random digging would never yield much useful information in person, being a better aid to other distant workings.

For using the techniques here in this book, for mind dowsing, you'll need to know each time what piece of information, or type of information, you're after. Also, because of the thought chaos just described, you'll have to make sure your subject is thinking of the thought you're after.

The thought you're looking for *must* be pulled forward, out of the chaos, for you to dowse it.

In contact mind reading, which is basically a training stepping stone to a real power, you had your subject keep something actively in his or her mind. You even had your subject think about objects with a specific focus—namely, something in the room, something on a table, something in the room your subject wants you to do something with. This same kind of focus is necessary for mind dowsing, although, as we'll see, the person you're reading doesn't necessarily have to know that such a thing is occurring.

When a thought is focused on by your subject, he or she makes it tangible on a mental level. It becomes something that you can sympathetically test with binary dowsing. Again, we come back to the principle of sympathetic attraction, or the simple fact that like attracts like in the unseen world. In ordinary dowsing this manifests in the age-old practice of carrying a small sample of what you are looking for, perhaps in a pocket. Dowsing for silver while wearing some, for instance, would put you in sync with silver's vibrations (or whatever you wish to call the unseen essence of something). You would then undergo the binary process of moving over each patch of suspect ground until you got a yes response; your ability at finding the element would only be strengthened by the sympathetic link.

In the same way, having a thought actively held in mind makes it sympathetically present. Limiting the amount of thoughts present helps, too, just as dowsing in a particular field for water is always better than walking the length of the country with a rod in hand! However, when reading someone's mind who is unaware of your intention, this becomes somewhat of a wild card. The best you can do is hope that by getting the person to think of the desired thought he or she will focus on it at least briefly enough to block all else out.

The best way to see these principles at work in mind reading is to try the art itself. We'll use modifications of the last chapter's experiments to do so. Once you get some experience at dowsing minds with a subject's knowledge, we'll explore how you can do it covertly.

Familiar Beginnings

Your experimentation with contact mind reading was marked by numerous attempts at seeking out subtle impulses from a subject's muscles. (And if you haven't experienced this yet, what are you waiting for? Get practicing!) After a few tries at Contact Experiment One, you likely began to feel some of the other sensations described in the last chapter. Namely, you began to feel that subtle pulling toward the object in your thoughts. In time, this pulling should have led you with increasing regularity to the right objects and actions throughout all three experiments. Yet the physical link was still there helping you. It's time to sever that link and awaken fully your inner potential.

To get your mind dowsing underway, you'll go back to doing Contact Experiment One . . . but remove the contact. The same will hold true as you advance through the other two. Rather than reiterate the three experiments given in the last chapter, I'll just say a few words about how to modify them to suit your new level of advancement.

You already know the first modification you'll be making. Once you feel confident enough to advance to mind dowsing, at no point in any of the three experiments should you make contact with your subject. You may hold your receiving hand, palm out, toward him or her at first, as this may help you concentrate. It might not do much to actually draw thoughts from the subject, but a psychodrama trigger can't hurt. However, in time, this gesture should be avoided, too, as you simply won't be able to pull it off in public without looking like a cop directing traffic, or without feeling way too self-conscious to concentrate.

Without cues from your receiving hand, the only thing you'll be feeling for during the experiments is that subtle pull I described in the last chapter. Whether you're circling the room with or seated next to the subject, that pull in your projecting hand is all that matters.

How did you feel the beginnings of this pull's development? Some sense this as a tingle when the hand is getting closer or moving in the right direction. Others feel an actual but subtle temperature change when they're on the right track, giving a whole new meaning to the phrase "getting warmer." Interestingly enough, you might feel either warmer or colder as you approach the right spot, or action, or thing, or whatever. When the pull manifests as a temperature change, it's not a specific type of temperature change you should be feeling for, but the fact that your hand is beginning to change temperature at all.

And not surprising is the fact that more than a few of you will feel the pull as an actual tug in the right direction or toward the right action. Such impulses may startle you, but they do make themselves known.

However you feel it, make certain you recognize the pull when it appears. Here's how to work with the pull in each modified training experiment:

When performing Contact Experiment One without contact, for the purpose of developing mind dowsing, you should still ask the person helping you to keep the object in the room in mind. However, without your holding his or her wrist, you won't be able to enjoy that symbiotic walk around the room where the subject seems to lead you (even though you were dragging him or her). You'll need to instead tell the subject that you will be moving around the room together in slow circles. Tell him or her to stop whenever they see you doing so. You'll be sweeping the room with your projecting hand, seeking the feeling that you've entered the right area. Zero in as normal, using the increasing strength of the pull as a guide.

For Experiment Two, the only modification is that you don't touch the subject. Still have him or her concentrate, and slowly move your hand over the objects lined up until one feels right—until the pull manifests.

By the time you've achieved contact-free success at the previous two experiments, consider trying Experiment Three without the aid of a walking subject. That is, have him or her enter a room, pick an object, then pick an action for you to perform with said object. Your subject should then sit in the center of the room, facing the door. His or her eyes can be open or closed, since they're not going to be fixed on any object as a giveaway. You should walk around the room, dowsing the objects as your subject concentrates.

No doubt, achieving success at even one of these contact-free experiments will amaze you. Making it through the modified third one will shatter all disbelief barriers and awaken in you an intuition you never dreamed possible.

Now, on to using your newfound ability in nightly life.

Probing Thoughts

A good term for contact-free mind reading is receptive telepathy. As the name implies, the desired effect is to be open or receptive to the thoughts of others. In true telepathy, both participants actively send and receive messages in a two-way fashion. Difficult to achieve, true telepathic communication requires that both participants have developed psychic skills to similar levels. In receptive telepathy, however, the work is all on one person, so to speak. The work is all accomplished through the arcane art of mind dowsing.

To use this power, to become a true mind reader, you have to develop your receiving skills as well as the ability to get your subject to send the desired thought.

This last sentence brings us back to one of the biggest secrets of mind reading: You often have to coax the right thought out of someone. Again, the thought must emerge from the chaos for you to find it.

In all your experimentation so far, you got your subjects to bring thoughts to the forefronts of their minds consciously and with the intention of helping you; they focused on objects, and they imagined actions performed with those objects. But it's also possible to get others to bring forth certain thoughts with the power of suggestion. Doing so is even possible from across a room!

Simple as it may seem, once you get your subject to think about his or her take on a specific idea, you can read this thought. Few people outside the magickal world really understand the power of thought. Cowans or those unaware of mystical practices use what goes on "upstairs" as a mere stepping-stone; to such individuals, thoughts are just part of a long process that can only be accomplished through physical means. "Think it, then do it" is the non-occult way.

Witches and other occultists make use of thought and willpower to create reality. We know that the mind is where creation begins, and that thoughts are tangible in many ways. Their tangibility makes them more than magickal tools—thoughts are real enough to be touched and examined from afar.

By now it might be clear that to access impressions from others you'll need to do two things: suggest and probe. Here are the secrets of each, in detail.

Sending Simple Suggestions

In chapter 12 we'll be dealing with the power of occult and hypnotic suggestion when used on others. For mind-reading purposes, however, you don't need to do anything quite so fancy. Right now we're concerned with the kind of suggestion that bombards us all daily. Ever walk into a room and feel comfortable, only to notice someone shivering? You very well might feel a sudden chill, even if you're dressed in a sweater and the other person is wearing a tee shirt—the suggestion may get through. Or, have you ever heard someone mention a song and then you get it stuck in your head for the rest of the night?

I'm sure you get the idea.

Advertisers rely on this subtle form of suggestion daily, trying to get you to feel hungry when you're not, trying to get you to think that you could never be cool enough in a social situation without drinking a particular beer.

Suggestion works. It's normal for the mind to fixate on a thought when an impulse comes in unexpected. If you were driving, for instance, you might not notice a tree go by on the side of the road; but you'd be thinking for some time about a branch that fell right in front of your car.

Yet we're not concerned with providing such startling impulses. For mind reading to work, the subject must only think of an idea for a few seconds—just long enough for you to probe the result.

Without getting into outright hypnosis, there are five ways to plant a suggestion, even though only two of these are worth pursuing in most cases. The five ways correspond to the physical senses. If someone sees, hears, smells, feels, or tastes something under the right circumstances, it will cause him or her to focus on the stimulus.

Of course, sight and sound are the best senses to work with in most cases. The other three have applications that will work in only rare situations. Clearly, it's not a good idea to just go around producing odors, or touching people, or sticking things into their mouths!

To use any of the senses to plant a suggestion, first decide what you want the person to think about. The right sense or combination of the senses will then be made obvious. If it's an abstract concept you want to get across, you will likely have to use sound—carefully chosen words. If it's an object, having it in hand would be a good idea; should you be the object, clearly there's nothing to carry.

Don't automatically rule out the other three senses. After you read how to use sight and sound, ideas might come to you for planting the others. Smell, for instance, has been proven to trigger memories better than any other sense, but it's difficult to make good use of in most scenarios.

Visual Cues

To use sight, you simply have to introduce a view of the object in a dramatic manner. Now, I don't mean you have to have custom club lighting and a smoke machine handy. Rather, you should be in control of when and how the person sees the object, and possibly you, for the first time.

Timing, surprise, and brevity are the keys to making a visual suggestion work.

You have to be certain that you have the person's attention when you want to introduce a visual cue. Don't miss what could be your one chance to get this right. After a botched suggestion, you'll have to wait at least a half hour or so before making another attempt, and how often are you guaranteed such an enduring audience with someone?

When you're sure the person is paying attention, show the object in an unexpected fashion. Just don't let the action become the focus of the suggestion. "Accidentally" producing a photo from a pocket while you're pretending to search for something else is fine; in this case be certain the person sees the image, then put it away. Taking the photo and extending your arm so the image almost touches the person's nose is not fine; the only suggestion planted here would be that you're a weirdo, and the photo would be quickly forgotten.

Notice I said you should put the photo away. Brevity is important, as a visual cue quickly fades into the background when it stays in sight, and questions about why you're brandishing it for such a long time may arise, and, again, your subject could come to some conclusions about your apparent weirdness. Something glimpsed quickly, at the right time and in the right manner, will linger . . .

. . . linger long enough for you to read one's thoughts about the object, of course.

If you're the object about which you want to gauge someone's thoughts, two similar but modified rules apply. First, you'll need to make eye contact; carefully select the initial time you let this occur. However, and this is important, do not try to get anything across in your own gaze! Go for pure neutrality—no smiles or frowns—but maintain a soft expression. Pay close attention to what you do with your brow and eyes. Do not squint or try to make your eyes seem in any way harsh. Keeping the thought in mind that you're doing something miraculous will help you maintain the right sense of mystique (more on mystique and magnetism in chapter 12).

After you've "appeared," vanish again if possible and try to plant yet another suggestion about five or ten minutes later. Should you be at a small social gathering, you'll have to make due with the first time, as it might be difficult for you to disappear for a while.

However you approach this, once the careful appearance of the object, or of you, has planted a suggestion, you can at that point proceed to use the mind dowsing technique taught later in this chapter.

Or, you can choose to supplement your suggestion with a verbal cue, if appropriate. Indeed, a verbal cue might be your only option if you're the object you want planted as a thought. This is because you can't always control the first time someone sees you, and the idea of trying is especially moot if the person knows you already.

What Words Are For

For whatever reason you turn to them, verbal cues can be powerful ways of planting suggestions. Even in hypnosis, the majority of suggestions are made via words and tone of voice, not by mysterious passes and swinging pocket watches on chains.

While visual cues can be flashed from across a room, verbal cues need to be made from either close up or possibly from another building or town. That is, you will have to engage the individual in even the most transient of conversation, be it in person or over the phone. It won't do to just shout out a suggestion. You need the individual to actually pay attention to what you say for the cue to sink in. And even if he or she listens to your sudden outburst, this person will likely end up thinking something unflattering.

You get the idea. A little subtlety goes a long way in the occult world. And it is with subtlety that you should deliver verbal cues.

Even though the goal is to bring a thought to the forefront of a person's mind, you should never ask a question outright. Getting someone to mull something over would make it very difficult for you to read what's going on in his or her head. Besides, a question begs an answer, and if you felt the person would answer . . . why would you bother with trying to read his or her mind?

You want the person's general thoughts on a subject to manifest as just that: thoughts. Answers to questions are not always honest. And were the person planning on telling you a lie to answer your question, you'd find it difficult to use his or her mind as a binary dowsing tool. It would be difficult to read past all the various spins on a story that he or she was considering giving you as a response.

The easiest way to verbally trigger a thought that you can then pick up is to be indirect. Make a statement, never pose a question, and make it a statement that *almost* demands a response. Select a verbal cue that might be perceived as "throwaway" chatter by the one you're trying to read. Make it something that would most likely result in an unspoken thought in the person. This resulting thought could range from sarcasm to amusement, from anger to joy. All that matters is that you choose words that elicit such a thought.

Getting across exactly what I mean here begs an example. Let's suppose you wanted to read someone's thoughts to determine if you were welcome at a certain event or place—perhaps it's a social function you suspect you were invited to as a result of guilt or perceived obligation. You would not want to say something like: "Great party. It was really cool of you to get in touch with me through Kate." Much better would be a statement that elicits an answer that requires no thought, only emotion—an answer that reveals true feelings. For instance, say something like: "Getting here was tough, but I made it." If someone really harbored any animosity toward you, the first thought to pop into his or her mind would be something to the effect of: "Too bad you did."

I can't really tell you exactly the type of statement to go for with a verbal cue, any more than I could tell you which type of visual cue would bring about the best response. It's something for which you'll have to rely on your own intuition in each case. Do remember your goal, however, and it won't be too hard to pull off a decent verbal cue.

Again, put simply, the goal is to get the person thinking about whatever nugget of information you're after. Plant a subtle, brief suggestion that accomplishes this, and make sure the statement is one unlikely to evoke a spoken response.

Remember: No questions!

How's that for a subtle suggestion?

Probing for Results

Okay, you've gotten your subject to think about whatever it is you want on his or her mind. What next?

Here's where things get strange: You're about to dowse the contents of your subject's mind as if they were objects floating in front of you.

Recall, thoughts are tangible. I mentioned this earlier not to be prosaic. As weird as the notion of dowsing thoughts like solid objects might seem at first, stick with me on this . . . at least until you give it a try.

Before you can access the other's thoughts on the topic you planted, you'll have to do a little thinking on this topic yourself. Even though you sent the suggestion in a visual way or as a statement, you'll have to now begin to think of it as a question you can pose to the dowsing mechanism, which is the combination of your trained mind and body and the other's mind.

See the issue at hand—the information you're dowsing for—as a question that can have one of two outcomes. Yes or no? Left or right? Like or dislike? Although with practice you can dowse people's views on questions with three or four possible outcomes, for now you should stick to basic binary. Something serious can work, such as: Does he think the contract will benefit his company—yes or no? As can something bordering on silly: Does she want me to take the red Skittle or the blue one?

Practice is practice, so in a way no experiment is too silly.

Once you've got your query figured out, assign some dowsable parameters to the possible answers. (Again, bear with me for a moment if this seems odd.) Make the possible answers into things that can float in the air before you.

Starting to see where we're going with this yet?

Imagine that "yes" is, for example, to the right, and that "no" is to the left. See the possible answers as words, or, if it's more appropriate, as colors or images hovering in the air.

The idea here will be to ask yourself which of these possible answers is the one reflecting the person's thoughts. It's almost as if you were doing Experiment Two again, but this time with invisible objects—invisible to everyone but you, of course.

Which brings us to an important point: Because only you know what you're doing, and because you should keep it that way, perform the following actions in a subtle manner.

Slightly extend your hand, perhaps just a finger or two. This should appear to someone watching as if you were about to raise a point but got interrupted.

Now, with your fingertips inches away from the two (for now) astral representations of possible choices or answers to your question, begin to move slowly back and forth over each, just as you did with physical objects in Experiment Two.

It's important to note that time is precious here. All the steps mentioned so far should happen within a second or two after you plant your suggestion. Then, with the phantom choices hovering before you, try to determine as quickly as possible which answer or object is the right one. Don't give the person you're reading from enough time to go off on a tangent!

If you've been working on the modified or contact-free experiments, you should know well the feel of the pull you're looking for here. Try to keep an open mind when dowsing the abstract thoughts in front of you. Only focus on the question, and not on what you think the most likely answer might be.

The answer will come.

Going Beyond Binary

I'm certain more than a few of you will want the option of expanding mind dowsing beyond the simple binary form presented so far. Indeed, once you get the basics down you should have no problem modifying the technique to suit most any kind of mind reading need. Some simple ways to ease into this multi-answer dowsing are presented here.

But first, a few words on something I didn't want you to dwell on before you finished reading how the basic art is performed. As straightforward as mind dowsing is, and as few steps as it contains, it won't always be able to tell if you got the right impression. Sure, you will get a result every time if you've been practicing long enough to sense the pull in your hand. However, you won't always have a way to verify if you were right. Taking our previous example of the social event, for instance, you would not want to say, "Ah-hah, so I'm not welcome here," considering that your host likely didn't say anything and was only sipping her drink as you probed her.

Sometimes, you'll have to take whatever results you get and act on them as you would act on a gut instinct. This is fine, but a little reinforcement from time to time is nice, too. Boosting your confidence can only boost your abilities.

Continue to experiment with friends for the instant gratification and reinforcement only they can provide. Use them to develop your skills to the point where you can select from far more than binary responses.

Feel free to modify the experiments that follow, depending on whom you get to work with you, and how silly or serious you want such sessions to be. These are only examples of some of the amazing things you can do with a little practice.

Simple Checkups

How "on" are your abilities today? Do a simple binary checkup to find out.

Relax with someone you trust and ask that person to think about something that has a binary answer. No need for suggestion here. Just outright ask the subject something that has a yes/no, choice A/choice B response.

Dowse for a result, and ask if you're right.

Pick a Number

Chances are, if you tell someone you're a mind reader, he or she will challenge you with "Oh, yeah? Well, what number am I thinking of?" Think of this experiment as a way to save someone the trouble of asking!

Ask your volunteer to think of a number from one to eight and to keep that number in mind. Then, imagine that numbers one through four are floating as a group to your left, and five through eight are lumped in a group to your right. Dowse to find out which group the person's number is in.

When you think you've got the right group, mentally divide the numbers into two pairs. Try to dowse for which pair holds the number.

Finally, split the two numbers in your mind, one to the left and one to the right. Which is the one your volunteer is thinking of? It will be easy to find out now.

Only ask for reinforcement (for example, "Is your number four?") after you think you've narrowed it down to the right one. Don't ask each step of the way, as it will distract you too much.

Pick a Number Again

Start out with a similar request as in the preceding experiment. This time, however, ask your volunteer to pick a number between one and nine.

Rather than break up the numbers into two sets at a time now, divide them into three groups of three. Dowse each of the three groups to find out whether the number is found within one through three, four through six, or seven through nine. Then dowse each of the numbers in your suspected group to find the right one.

Again, only ask for reinforcement when you're sure you've got the right number.

Mind Reading A to Z

Ask your volunteer to think of a letter from *A* through *Z.* Break the alphabet into two groups—*A* through *M* and *N* through *Z*—and dowse each group to find where the letter is located.

Now comes the real test of your dowsing patience (and visualization ability). See as clearly as possible, in your mind's eye, the letters in the suspect group. You can do this one letter at a time, or line them up and move your hand across them. You will have to test each to see if it pulls your hand, identifying itself as the chosen letter.

Narrowing down twenty-six to one in this fashion will give you a morale boost like no other.

These simple experiments should give you wonderful practice until you can advance to pulling much more impressive thoughts from the minds of others.

For now, however, it's time to take immediate advantage of all the psychic skills you've been developing—time to take your workings with the unseen and apply them to the physical world.

Magickal miracles await you in part three.

Part Three

Nocturnal Magick

Chapter Nine

Altering Reality: Simple Spells and Rites

Nocturnal Witchcraft is a religion with special prerequisites, as we've seen. Appreciating the current is only possible by getting to know the Gods and Goddesses of Night, through the ways discussed in part one. The Dark Craft is also only accessible by those willing to undergo the special mental training explored in part two.

All these prerequisites ready you for the final stage of your developmental path: making magick.

In every way, this chapter is an introduction to the art of mystically creating change in the universe. Certain occult principles apply to all types of magick, pagan or not, dark or light. Once you master them, the principles can be applied to our tradition with amazing results.

And that's what part three is all about: results.

Manifestation

When people hear the word manifestation within a mystical context, they often think of something that appears out of nowhere. But magickal results arrive only as a result of careful planning and a cause worth expending energy for. And magickal or occult results only enter your immediate surroundings or personal reality through natural laws.

As powerful as the techniques you're about to learn are, please do not expect them to violate the harmonious way in which the universe operates. The God and Goddess set forth a terrific place for us to learn and grow as incarnated souls. Certain limitations will always surround us, as will certain seemingly uncontrollable circumstances and probabilities. However, we can bend all these factors from time to time. We can use magick to manipulate reality in subtle ways that bring about fantastic results.

Have you ever checked out a piece of fiction involving the concept of time travel? Whether it's a book or movie, the story invariably touched on the idea that if even the slightest thing is changed in the past, the future will be drastically altered.

Consider what could happen if you accidentally swatted a mosquito during a visit to the Middle or Dark Ages. You may end up, as a result, coming back to a modern time where some madman has taken over the world. Why? What if the mosquito was supposed to make some woman ill, preventing her from meeting some man, falling in love, and eventually starting a family line that ends up in said madman's birth?

A chain of seemingly innocuous events like these can result in something major. The universe works by cause and effect. Once an initial cause starts a chain of events rolling, the final effect can be miraculous or disastrous.

But the initial cause does not always have to be out of our control. Neither are we powerless against stepping in to alter an event flow that's leading to an undesirable result. Using your will to set a desirable chain of events in motion, or to change an undesirable chain that is in motion, is a practical definition of magick.

You may never be able to differentiate which of these is the case, of course. At any given moment are you really setting forth a new series of events or altering one? It can be argued that there is one primal cause, one initial domino that was tipped by the Source to set off all the chain reactions we're still experiencing. We can also make a case for the fact that each circumstance brings about new chances for the universe's inhabitants to create their own tomorrows. Either way, we can step in and twist how the dominoes fall along the way.

While magick cannot work against physical laws, it can manipulate probability. It can create wonderful coincidences. It can attract helpful synchronicity into our lives. Like the hypothetical mosquito that held the fate of civilization in its decision to bite or not, magick can create undeniable change in the world, even if it manifests as the tiniest event or impulse.

And there's that root word again: manifest.

How is it possible to make something seemingly appear from nothing? By understanding the mechanics of magick and making them work for you—it's that simple.

Mastery of the prerequisites in parts one and two will help you master these mechanics. True, an understanding of the Gods and the enhancement of your mental powers provide their own benefits, but they will now help you create powerful change, too. We'll get to how your relationship with the God and Goddess will help in a moment; but first, down to the basics that will occur in your mind.

Mind Manipulating Matter

Every act begins in the mind. We think of what we wish to do, then we do it. Simple, this concept, yet magick is not much different. The only reason people don't cast spells as often as they act on the desire to sit in a chair, for instance, is that with magick our minds need to not only take care of the planning but some of the doing as well.

Before casting a spell or performing a ritual, we decide upon some need—we begin to imagine in an undisciplined manner what we wish to accomplish. I say "undisciplined" because in the planning phases of a physical act we wouldn't sit in some dark room and try to intensely create an image of our goal using something like part two's visualization exercises. Whatever images pop into our heads during ordinary thought would serve well to help establish a goal. This is the mind working in its typical planning role that it also performs when deciding on a mundane or nonmystical course of action.

Now comes the magick. After a goal is set, a Witch can use the power of the mind's sympathetic link in the universe: the mental plane.

All reality is composed of three layers of planes that coexist with each other. Two of these—the mental and astral—are subtle or intangible; the other is physical, and named such. Manifestation is accomplished when a thought is made to work or progress through these planes.

The mental plane is accessed by our minds at all times. This is a formless realm where our thoughts, mystical and mundane, can be born.

The astral plane is the formative realm. Here our abstract thoughts can begin to take shape, and we can empower certain thoughts to take shape without any physical help from us (that is, we can do magick).

The physical plane is where creation occurs. This is where our shaped thoughts can take on tangible substance either through our actions or the final results of mystical manifestation.

Here are two quick examples of how the planes work for mundane and mystical manifestation:

To buy a house, you would imagine or think (mental plane) of the type of place you're seeking. Next, you would start to imagine a course of action (astral plane) that could get you in such a house. Finally, you would go out to physically enact the course of action, thereby buying the house (physical plane). If you didn't have the money, however, you might want to . . .

. . . cast a spell for money. To do so, you would at some point think of how much cash you need (mental). You would then imagine yourself with the money, empowering this thought (astral). The money would then, through natural means, manifest in your life (physical).

Sticking to the mystical example, how do you think the money will manifest? Magick only works with physical laws, remember. You won't find a sack with a dollar sign on it materializing on your kitchen table. What you ask for will come into your life via natural means.

And you will get exactly what you ask for, which is why you have to be careful what you ask for, and how you ask for it. The money in our example could come from a court settlement . . . perhaps after you've broken your legs on an icy sidewalk. Is that how you wanted to collect some cash? Disasters can abound with poorly planned magick. Another example—cast a flippant spell to attract some new love, and you may end up bringing an obsessive or dangerous mate into your life.

Why such negative possibilities? It's not that the universe is sadistic. Rather, it takes the path of least resistance to fulfilling your wishes. And sometimes this path is not a positive one, because of the forces that happen to be at work in your life at the time. To avoid getting burned by your magick, you have to always design rites that bring things to you for the greater good (more on this in a moment).

Going back to our money spell example, let's consider how you'd want to design the rite so that cash came your way without calamity. The idea is to bend the right kind of probabilities with your thought-forms, which you'll build on the astral plane. With money magick done properly, maybe you'll win a contest, be offered a low-interest loan, or even find some cash you lost. Much nicer ways to have your magick manifest, no?

Whether you've been exposed to different types of magick over the years through practice or friends or even through the scanning of shelves in the New Age section, you should be able to search your memory now and see how all those diverse practices follow the simple path of manifestation just described. Planning (mental), visualization and empowerment (astral) of some kind, and results (physical) are always present, whether you're working with candles, herbs, or even spirits. Any book that tells you to simply read a few lines and wait for a result is not teaching magick—fantasy, yes, but not magick.

All the techniques taught in part three somehow work through the planes to accomplish a goal. It's the particular "somehow" in each case for which you have to learn to use a magickal technique. That will be the focus of all the pages that follow: revealing the mechanics of creating miracles in different ways.

In different, dark ways.

Help from the Gods

Before we start with our first method for manifesting a desire, let's briefly revisit a practice that can bring great power to any Witch's magick: the calling of the Gods.

Recall the two types of invocation? One, the simple type involving a recited call, is fine for hasty magick, in much the same way as it's fine for just quickly communing with the Gods or praying. It can put you in the right mood and can let the God or Goddess smile upon your rite. However, you get out of invocation and magick what you put into them.

True invocation or godform assumption—that's the way to provide your rite with a stronger power source . . . with the power of the Source itself, that is.

We're not going to revisit the entire technique taught in chapter 3. Rather, I'm just going to reinforce three ideas here.

First, select the right God or Goddess to call upon. This is especially critical if you are doing a full assumption. Using appendix A and any other relevant sources, be certain to pick a deity that is attributed to the energies you're trying to work with. Do not call on Persephone for a healing, for instance, but do call upon Hecate if you wish to banish the illness.

Second, remember to call upon the God or Goddess in a way that reflects your need. Do not use a generic invocation—write one specific to the working at hand.

Finally, go with whatever the God or Goddess inspires you to do. Most times, the ritual will proceed as you planned, with the feeling of the deity's proximity enhancing it. But on occasion the God or Goddess may want to provide you with a variation or a new technique that's right for you at the time. One of the greatest aspects of Witchcraft in general is that the Gods are close to us within ritual. Relish this and, in Nocturnal Witchcraft, relish the similar nature these deities have to you.

They want to see you succeed, both with your development and your magick.

Writing Rites

Just as you will write many custom invocations to call upon specific Gods for specific purposes, you will also have to write a great number of custom spells in your life as a Witch. While chants and the like that you find in books are fine if they feel right to you, it's easiest in most cases to write ones on your own that accurately get across what you're trying to do in a ritual.

Remember, just reciting some words will never result in successful magick. But coupled with the techniques taught here in part three, the words you write will have real power and create real change when uttered or intensely imagined in the mind's ear (the concept of saying something "to yourself").

Think of the words of a spell as a declaration of intent. They help keep your subconscious on track during the magickal part of a rite. While you're visualizing, empowering an object, whatever, the words strengthen the mystical act and make it clear to both you and the universe how things should play out. It is the words of a spell that can ensure no harm will come to you or anyone else as a result of the probabilities you are about to bend for your needs.

So, before you use any of the magick in this part of the book, it's clear you'll need to write a usable spell. Where to begin?

For starters, decide upon a need. In the invocation you do before a spell, you will only need to be general in that you need help with money, love, and so on. That's fine, but to write the spell that follows the invocation you will have to distill this need into a concrete statement, perhaps consisting of a few short phrases that identify why you want this result, what the approximate result should be, and maybe who it should affect and when you'd like it to manifest. Note that I didn't mention the "how" of a ritual—the path of modified probabilities that lead to manifestation is for the universe to decide.

You will be jotting this need statement on some scrap paper for now. For example, a money spell need statement might go like this: "I need help paying next month's rent. I desire eight hundred dollars. I want the money to arrive by the first of October." In a healing, your series of chosen statements would obviously include for whom the healing is being done. Make sure you only use another's name in a spell if you're sending the recipient something he or she would welcome. In a love spell, for instance, you should never mention another's name—heavy karmic penalties abound for trying to control another, even if you feel you're bringing him or her the wonderful gift of you!

These statements you jot down are not your spell. They're a brainstorming session for now. You will be rewriting these words directly into your spell's structure.

Start your spell with a comment that reinforces the presence of the Gods. Even though your invocation makes it clear you're calling for help with a specific aspect of your life, it helps immensely to reinforce the deity's involvement in the spell.

The next thing to do is write the body of the spell to reflect the technique you will be using. The myriad ways you can do this will become clear to you as you learn each of the techniques taught here in part three. But until you learn more about the mechanics of each mystical technique, the best way to master spell-writing basics for now is through example. We'll take the money spell statement just used and tie it to the structure of the Nocturnal Candle rite that follows in the next section. Simple and powerful, this rite, as you'll see, lets you charge a candle in a way you've never encountered in any candle magick book.

Here's one way you could mold your money-requesting words for the Nocturnal Candle rite:

In the presence of the Lady of Night,
I call upon the dark ether to coalesce and help me pay next month's rent.
Help me, Goddess, to bring the eight hundred dollars I need into my life.
May this candle's flame send out my request; may my request be
answered before October 1.
May this be carried out with harm to none, for the greater good.
So mote it be.

Note that I added a line that ensures the spell will bring no harm to you or others. This is the final step, and perhaps the most important. To avoid it is to invite disaster. I'm not kidding about this. While the universe won't always try to manifest things in a destructive fashion, a strong need coupled with an uncontrolled ritual could achieve strong results . . . at any cost. So don't tempt chaos. Add the line I put in the example, or add one similar to it. This way, you can put all your power into a ritual without fear of retribution.

I also added "so mote it be," which is a traditional Craft line that helps establish to your mind that you have completed something your will and the universe should carry out.

Your written spells may be more poetic or shorter and punchier than the example just given. That's fine. Use whatever style works for you. And by that, I mean whatever spell style actually *works* for you.

Magick does work, as you'll see.

A Three-Minute Spell

Regardless of how many advanced techniques you master in the occult world, you won't always have time to put them to use. For this reason, I include the following three-minute spellcasting technique that can serve as much more than just an introduction to magick. It's a technique you may find yourself using even after the gates of the Underworld have opened for you!

Whenever possible, perform this Nocturnal Candle rite in a magick circle. That is, cast the circle up to step twenty-five, invoking a deity appropriate to your rite, and proceed. If you're in a true hurry, do a quick banishing and simple invocation (still of an appropriate God or Goddess), then begin the rite. Either way, keep in mind the tangibility of night that holds the form of your sacred space. This concept, on which you normally mediate in step six of the circle-casting, will play a factor in the Nocturnal Candle rite.

The only things you need to conduct the rite are a spell you've written following the criteria discussed earlier, a black taper with candleholder, and matches or a lighter. You can do the rite on your altar, if it's available, or any table or flat chair bottom (this is a great spell for travelers).

Of course, the rite should really only be performed at night.

The Nocturnal Candle

With your sacred space created somehow, and God or Goddess invoked, pick up the black taper with your receiving (likely your left) hand.

Walk clockwise to the easternmost edge of your circle (regardless of whether it was cast or only formed as a sphere in the banishing). See, with your mind's eye, how the darkness presses against the edge of your sacred space, helping it maintain the sphere or circle. Say:

Behold the tangible ether of night, which holds in it all possibilities.

Extend your arm to touch the edge of the circle with the candle, and walk clockwise, keeping your arm extended. Imagine that the ether of night is being absorbed into the candle. You are helping this occur by using your receiving hand. However, do not try to pull the ether into yourself. Only feel the energy pulsing within the candle. While you're moving around the circle and feeling all of this, say:

As I draw the power of night into this candle, I prepare to manifest my need.

Return to the spot at the east where you began and pull the charged candle away from the edge of the circle. Move clockwise to your standard starting spot with your altar or table before you.

Put the taper in a candleholder. Imagine with your eyes open that it is glowing in the same way a skrying mirror would. Imagine that it is glowing with the same kind of slightly lighter darkness, if you will, that you often see within your nocturnal portal.

Imagine your need being fulfilled. See yourself already having whatever it is you're about to ask for (but do not imagine any steps that may result in having your need fulfilled).

Hold your open projecting hand in front of the candle, with your palm facing the taper.

Read or recite the spell you wrote, still imagining, with eyes open, your need fulfilled. As you read the words, begin to raise emotional energy as discussed in chapter 5 (do so without thinking of any memories, of course—by now you should have mastered this). Tense your muscles to help the energy-raising along.

Try to reach your energy peak either as you utter the last line of the spell or right after. Take a deep breath and exhale, blasting the energy out through your right hand and into the absorbing candle.

Light the wick.

Try to imagine for a moment that the flame is sending out both the absorbed essence of night and the charge that you put into the candle. But don't think of your need at this point, or any more this evening, in fact.

If you cast a circle, perform the closing, including the treat and drink. Otherwise, go and do something grounding, such as eating or having a conversation about nonmystical things.

Place the candle in a safe place where it can burn itself out.

Your need will be fulfilled.

Chapter Ten

Dreaming for Change

Dreams can do more than just deliver us inspiration by night. Although the majority of these mind movies involve us passively viewing their contents, it is possible to occasionally take the reins of a dream.

The concept of conscious or lucid dreaming is hardly new. Techniques for "waking up" within a dream and taking control of it have been around for hundreds of years in most parts of the world, with some cultures possibly having been aware of the practice thousands of years ago. Modern psychology caught on with some vigor to lucid dreaming in the latter half of the twentieth century.

The benefits of waking up within a dream seemed to be many. By realizing one is dreaming, he or she could turn the night movie into most anything. The enactment of fantasies, the possession of superhuman abilities such as flight, the chance to step outside the limitations of the physical world—all were promises of lucid dreaming.

However, while numerous mass-market paperbacks and magazine articles tried to excite the public about lucid dreaming, it never really took off as a practice. People would try it and have to keep at it for quite a while to obtain success. Even then, the ratio of successes to failures was seldom favorable, causing more than a few dreamers to move on to the pursuit of other interests. Why? People are not as reliant on mind fantasies as the proponents of lucid dreaming believed. When it comes to a technique requiring mental discipline and practice, we want to get something useful out of it.

I saw an ad in the late 1980s for a lucid dreaming aid that showed a sleeping cartoon man with thought bubbles around him; in these bubbles he was surrounded by beautiful women who were diving through a sunken Spanish galleon, and, get this, dancing in mounds of gold! The ad went so far as to say something like, "Hey, get out of the rut of your daily life and live your fantasies every night." Even a man intrigued by such a silly ad, however, likely became quickly irritated by how those women were never there when he awoke, and how any artifacts he found under the sea and any gold coins he stuck in his pockets were long gone when sunlight sliced through the cracks of his eyelids.

Further, even those who were content to just live out their adventures in dreams found another annoying problem in the whole process. Most lucid dreaming techniques relied on you realizing you were dreaming and then taking control of the dream. The problem? When you realized you were dreaming, you usually got so excited that at most you could tell yourself to fly or head over to a fun imaginary nightclub before you woke up—hardly an experience worth all the effort. And even if they could maintain the lucid state, these dreamers did so after having been asleep. Lucid dreaming goals cannot exactly be remembered. Think about it. When you wake in the morning, into the real world, you probably have a hard enough time remembering what it is you wanted to accomplish this day. Imagine waking into a lucid dream and trying to remember a fantasy goal you set for yourself before turning in!

But is lucid dreaming really useless to us in the waking world? Or does it provide us another way to interact with the power of the night?

It all depends on which type of lucid dreaming you're talking about. Before we get into the secret of which type of lucid experiences can actually be put to good occult use, let's consider the potential of the dream state itself.

A Shortcut to the Astral

Consider just how effective our imaginative faculties are while we dream. We can see visions of a sort in startling clarity, even if they sometimes don't make sense. Dreamtime is when even a neophyte can visualize perfectly. The mind's eye is truly the only eye at work.

There's more to this time than just a fantasy light show, however. A concept I've come across repeatedly and have found to be true is that during dreams our astral bodies sometimes travel. I've had numerous out-of-body experiences that have been initiated in the dream state. I know I'm not alone in this, but even if you haven't had such an experience, don't worry. The frequency of such experiences in certain individuals shows us that there is some connection between the dream state and the astral plane. Yes, that astral plane—the one that figures in magickal workings.

Recall, manifestation goes from the mental plane, to the astral, to realization in the physical. Therefore, if we can set our minds to some magical goal (mental plane) and activate this thought during a dream, when we can powerfully visualize and give the goal form (astral), then it will manifest (physical).

This is just another example of how in its purest form, magick is about creating thoughtforms—literally a thought given form, first astrally then physically. The Nocturnal Candle rite got you started on this, having you imagine a simple goal for the candle's gathered etheric energy to then fuel. The techniques in this and the next chapter continue developing your abilities at making thoughts into reality . . . your abilities at thereby altering reality.

Were the ancients aware of this? Some certainly were.

In the East, the Tibetan monks would train using a dream manual that taught them how thoughtforms are created in the dream state. We'll be touching on techniques based on their powerful magick in a few instances in the pages that follow.

Other parts of the world contain a few interesting examples of dreaming for change. The Senoi of Malaysia would change forms that appeared in their dreams and even attack intimidating ones to help create a waking reality they desired. Too, every culture with shamans has record of a similar practice, where the shaman would enter some inner dreamlike state to confront various forces and either ask them for help or coax said forces into making change.

Some of the dreamers of yesteryear would also perform something called dream incubation. This practice of trying to coax a certain type of dream seems to have its roots in Mesopotamia, and later enjoyed widespread use throughout the ancient world, including Greece. While not always intended to create magickal change, an incubated dream can result in the delivery of certain types of useful information; this makes dream incubation more like the practice of listening to the night (covered back in chapter 6) than that of random dream interpretation. Dream incubation was often used to attain visions of the Gods in ancient times. To do the latter, a dreamer would often physically travel first to a sacred spot or temple associated to a particular deity.

We'll be exploring how to use all these types of ancient techniques in this chapter. How will so many fit in this space? You'll be surprised to see just how much they have in common, how much of their techniques you already know, and how easy they will be for you to implement, nightkind.

Having Real Lucidity in Lucid Dreaming

As hinted at just a couple of pages back, realizing that you're dreaming after you've been asleep for hours won't do much for you. Chances are you'd never be able to remember a particular course of mundane action to take, let alone a mystical one. So, unless you're interested in just having some short, strange dreams, don't spend any time worrying about or developing your ability to achieve a lucid dream while already asleep.

Fortunately, as mystics the world-round have found, there are benefits to entering a dream with consciousness intact. Some would argue that this is all an out-of-body experience is—just a lucid dream that you enter rather than wake up within. I argue staunchly that astral travel is so much more.

To enter a lucid dream from waking consciousness, you have to rely on your ability to first maintain consciousness at the edge of sleep or during the alpha brainwave state. Luckily, you already have some practice doing so. Remember the autosuggestion for mystical power taught in chapter 5? The diagonally descending flashes of color you visualized during that technique helped lull you into just these kinds of brainwaves. Applying this technique with a particular kind of suggestion statement will greatly help you enter a lucid dream from the waking state, as we'll see.

Starting your attempt at the right time will help, also. The greatest amount of dreaming activity takes place toward the end of psychic quiet time. This is the best time to attempt entering a dream from waking, too. If you've gone to bed early, set an alarm for about 4:30 A.M., or simply stay up until this approximate time. Either way, you'll be drowsy and able to easily produce alpha brain waves.

The drowsy condition you'll find yourself in before you fall asleep is conducive to visualization. More precisely, before you can get to the first stages of sleep or the theta brainwave state, you must first pass from beta (awake) down through the lowest frequency of alpha waves. And these low alpha waves result in what are known as hypnagogic images—the vivid, brief pictures that may make you jump while you're trying to drift off on a given night.

But it need not be such a chaotic time, this hypnagogic state of free-flowing imagery. You can also control what you see. With practice, most anything you think of during this state will appear clearly in your mind's eye.

Because of both the visualization boost it provides and the fact that you'll be able to do something with the dream state immediately following it, the hypnagogic is powerful. For Witches in training, it's an ideal time to experiment with thoughtforms, as well as with creating change by night.

Let's now take a look at how to send out two different types of thoughtforms—one to create magickal change in the waking world, and one to summon a particular type of information.

Dream Magick

The dream rite we're about to get to, as well as the one for dream incubation that's described later on, need not be done in a fully cast Nocturnal Circle. Besides the simple logic against getting up and going through a series of motions and words before trying to get some sleep, dream rites operate in a different way from other magickal rituals. Dream rites don't rely on a traditional use of power, from the raising to the manipulation to the release of it, and do not need the circle for focus. Further, a magick circle is designed to create a place outside time and space—dreams handle that on their own quite nicely.

The only thing you'll need to perform a dream spell is a spell that is written out. This should follow, for the most part, the tips presented in the previous chapter, with one modification to the body of the spell that we'll get to in a moment.

For starters, your spell should begin with at least one invoking line. This can be a request for the help of the God and/or Goddess in general, or it can be a call to a particular deity of Night Personified, like Hypnos (see appendix A).

Next, use as many lines in the body of the spell as it takes to get across all the nuances of your magickal need.

Follow your magickal need descriptions with a line that explains the form the spell will take. Say something to the effect of: "This request I shall send out through the realm of dream."

Now for the modification to spell structure. You'll also need one more line for dream magick. This extra line should be a condensation of all your statements of desire into one mantra, kind of like a phrase you'd use with the autosuggestion rite from chapter 5. It's okay to use some of the same words from the body of your spell. Just make certain the line is something short and easy to repeat, and write it in a positive way. For example, if your spell were to go into all the reasons of why you would like to have help in preparing for an important exam, your mantra line should not be something like "I hope to do well on my test." Rather, "I will excel at my coming exam" is better, and perhaps "I excel at math (or whatever subject)" might be best, being in the present tense. Whenever possible, your statement should be worded as if you have already achieved the goal.

End your written spell with the line or lines you use to ensure no harm comes to any as a result of your magick.

There's no need to memorize your written spell. You will only have to commit the mantra line to memory. Have on your nightstand a low power light for reading the entire spell. Candlelight is always better, of course, but unless you have a safe black candle such as a seven-day glass one, don't risk the possibility of your falling asleep with an open flame in the room.

If you choose to do the spell when it is most effective (again, toward the end of psychic quiet time), you will have to approach this in one of two ways: either you'll need to remain awake all night, which is certainly doable if you've nowhere to go the next morning, or you'll have to set an alarm for some time around 4:30 A.M. or so. Whichever you choose, make sure you're calm at this approximate time of predawn. If waking from an alarm, particularly if you've been up until a decent hour (1 or 2 A.M.) before settling down, you'll be ready to sink into sleep almost immediately after turning off the alarm. However, if you've been up all night only through the help of black coffee, perhaps dream magick won't work so well for you in such a wired state.

The spellcasting technique that follows contains a modification of a method that Tibetan monks use for entering a kind of lucid dream. What's more practical about the technique that follows, however, is that you do not have to succeed in having a complete lucid dream for the spell to work. You'll see what I mean by this in a moment.

In bed with the spell literally in hand, you're ready to begin.

Casting a Dream Spell

Turn on your lamp or light your glass candle.

Read your spell as loudly as you can. If someone is in bed with you or even in another bed in the same room, you might have to whisper. If possible, try to avoid having to say the spell in your mind only. Hearing your voice at this time will have a very powerful effect on your subconscious mind. Besides, imagining the words in your mind might help you get to sleep a little too soon if you're tired enough.

Turn off the lamp or blow out the candle and immediately get as comfortable as possible.

With eyes still open, begin to imagine a small (golf ball sized) silver sphere nestled inside your throat. Know it's there, and feel the almost warming sensation its permeating glow is producing on your entire neck.

Say out loud (if possible) the mantra line from your spell once more, and close your eyes, concentrating on seeing the silver sphere with greater clarity.

Repeating the mantra with your mind's voice, continue to focus on the sphere with your mind's eye.

Now for the tricky part. With your consciousness likely already slipping, you will have to try to concentrate on seeing images within the sphere, almost as if it were a crystal ball. What are you looking for? Images that are related to your goal. But don't gaze or simply wait for visions to appear. Forcefully see yourself, via the sphere, having accomplished whatever it is you're asking for, or imagine said desire coming ever closer toward you within the silver field of vision. Whatever feels right should work as an image, but do keep it simple enough to see clearly, quickly.

Keep repeating your mantra to yourself as you see the visions in the sphere. And, this is extremely important, keep imagining that the sphere is in your throat. This energy center will help you maintain consciousness as you enter the dream state.

In the hypnagogic state, the images you see will be vivid ones. They may also be fleeting ones, however. If you find they tend to change, that's fine, as long as you actively keep them "on track" whenever they shift into silly imagery that has nothing to do with the magickal goal at hand. If you let the images go any which way, you'll find yourself in a normal dream, your spell won't work, and you will miss out on a powerful experience.

That experience? All magick has a release point, when you send the energy out to do its work. If you've been repeating the mantra, seeing the images, and knowing that you're seeing them within a sphere inside your throat, this release point will come soon. You will find yourself in a lucid dream, fully aware of your mystical actions, yet asleep.

See the silver sphere moving out from your throat, passing through your neck, and out into the vista of the dream. Then observe what happens. You may very well receive some kind of large vision showing the magick beginning its work. I call this a reinforcing vision, which helps break down any belief barriers that your mind may put up against the possibility of real magick being done on this particular night.

It's okay if after the thoughtform goes out the dream soon engulfs you and lucidity fades. The dream spell is released and working. You can rest at this point.

A couple of quick tips regarding the preceding rite:

Know that you won't always be able to enter a lucid dream. This ability will come and go from night to night, depending largely on how awake or alert you are and what happened on a given day. If you have a strong magickal need and can't wait to attempt the rite again, try releasing the sphere thoughtform out into the field of your hypnagogic inner vision. This may still work just perfectly, although you might not see any visual indication that your spell has been sent out (and this reinforcing vision does have wondrous effects on how fast your need will materialize).

Also, if you need to do this kind of spell when you're not particularly tired, you could try doing part of the autosuggestion rite from chapter 5 first. Go through the steps to the point where you visualize the final, violet sphere. You can then perform the three deep breath cycles, but disregard the rest of the autosuggestion. Instead, proceed to open your eyes and begin casting the dream spell. As this isolated part of the autosuggestion that takes you through the descending colors will help lower your brainwave state, it's a wonderful aid to getting closer to the hypnagogic.

Summoning a Dream

You already know how to do this.

To be more specific, you know the two techniques that, slightly modified, make up dream incubation. Now it's time to practice them in this modified amalgam, and invite some meaningful dreamscapes into your life.

As we started discussing earlier in this chapter, the ancients used the practice of incubating a specific type of dream to receive helpful spiritual and mundane information and even to commune with the Gods. We can accomplish the same today. With such summoned dreams, you can go to sleep with a question and wake with a truly eye-opening answer. And you can do more than invoke the God and Goddess with dream incubation—you can seemingly spend hours in an ancient temple with them, enjoying inspiring conversation by the firelight of braziers.

I won't comment any further on how to apply the experience. Trust your intuition on this. You know what dream visions you need in your life this night, and when the sun next sets as well.

Dream Incubation

Set an alarm to ring in about three hours.

Lie down in bed with no lights on. Say:

Lord and Lady of Night, lend me your wisdom in dream tonight. Unseen ones,
let your presence break through the veil of sleep.

(Here, insert a special mantra: Either ask a question by saying,
"Reveal to me . . ." or ask the Gods to be with you by saying,
"Be with me as avatars tonight.")

Perform the deep relaxation, with eyes open.

Begin to achieve some inner quiet.

With eyes still open, begin to imagine a small silver sphere nestled inside your throat, just as with a dream spell. Know the sphere is there, feel it.

Repeat the mantra out loud (again, either a question or a request for the Gods to be with you). Close your eyes, concentrating on seeing the silver sphere with greater clarity.

Repeating the mantra to yourself, continue to focus on the sphere visualization. But do not try to see any images within the sphere. Just focus on the sphere for about three or four minutes, repeating the mantra.

Before you feel yourself slipping to the lowest alpha waves and the hypnagogic, raise up a tiny amount of emotional energy, repeat the mantra silently once more, and see the silver sphere dissolving, spreading its light through your body.

Try to think of nothing from this point, and await sleep.

Your incubated dream will come.

And you will remember this mystical experience, this dreamscape, as the alarm will wake you soon enough. You might want to have a pen and paper handy to document the nocturnal vision.

Chapter Eleven

Advanced Thoughtforms

Let the dark miracles manifest.

You are about to move into an area of study and practice that transcends all manner of spell and ritual you have ever encountered. When mastered by some, the techniques you're about to learn allow for true reality manipulation, for the achieving of results that seem to violate physical laws (only *seem* to, of course).

If you've ever desired to have three wishes, you're about to learn how to attain an infinite number of them. If you've ever truly wanted to create change in conformity with your will, read on.

What you learn in this chapter may be the last mystical technique you will ever feel the need to master.

Aims as life-changing as theurgy can be achieved through powerful magick—use this dynamo to bring yourself closer to the Source. Powerful magick can help with the little things, too, as well as the big things that come up now and again, yet which have no bearing on our development . . . at least none that we can make out yet.

Powerful magick can help us do *anything*.

Powerful magick is the masterful use of thoughtforms—literally, thoughts given form.

Manifestation.

Fantastic Phantasms

I've said this before and will swear on it unless all mystical experience is ripped from me (and Goddess may that never happen!): All the motions and words of ritual, all the material trappings from candles to daggers, are completely unnecessary. Unnecessary after a point, that is.

The psychodrama of ritual is only needed to break down the barriers our waking consciousness poses to our connection with unseen forces. If that's all you learn from this book, and you keep it in mind when training for other types of ritual work, you're destined to achieve all you seek from the unseen.

Of course, you're more than welcome to use this principle to activate the mysteries located within these pages, as well.

We'll be delving more on the idea of shattering belief barriers in the next section. For now, consider a side of this tenet you might not have dwelled on before.

If ritual is just psychodrama, then all magick is really mind magick. And all mind magick is, in actuality, mind power unleashed.

So, despite this being a Witchcraft book, I'd be remiss to not give at least a couple of brief examples of famous thoughtforms created by pure mind power. Then I'll show you how I have done and how you can do the same with some psychodramatic, magickal trappings.

The art of creating thoughtforms just may have been perfected by the monks in Tibet. As related in the wonderful book *Magic and Mystery in Tibet*, by Alexandra David-Neel (see Suggested Reading), certain ascetic monks spend time developing the ability to not only give form to thought, but to give immediate, tangible reality to their thoughtforms!

David-Neel has written in the aforementioned book and other books about how the monks could create even buildings that would protect one from the elements. Some thoughtforms, according to her, can even incarnate as living people, called *tulkas*. Now, this is all a bit hard to accept in our Western world, but it introduces the concept of thoughtforms that can learn to think for themselves (more on sentient or thinking thoughtforms later on).

More practical and believable is the practice the monks have of heating their bodies and remaining in the snow without any bundles of clothing. This is an excellent example of using thought to affect physical matter.

Some would argue that it's hard to take David-Neel's words with any less than a grain silo full of salt. The events occurred in a distant land—how convenient, right? All the phenomena cannot be so easily dismissed, however. For starters, scientists have measured amazing increases in monk body temperature. And, having seen the efficiency of the Tibetan techniques by practicing some of the more accessible ones, I'd have to argue in support of what's found in *Magic and Mystery in Tibet*. You might make the same endorsements, soon.

Still, for those who don't trust the mysteries of isolated mountains, there are examples of tangible thoughtform creations closer to home. Perhaps the most famous is related in the book *Conjuring Up Philip*, by Iris Owen and Margaret Sparrows (see Suggested Reading). Here we move away from the possibly subjective word of one traveler to the objective evidence of many.

The book relates how in 1973 eight members of the Society of Psychical Research in Toronto decided to think up a deceased spirit. No one in the group claimed to have any supernatural powers. They were four ordinary housewives (including Owen and Sparrows) and four ordinary working men—an accountant, an engineer, an industrial designer, and a scientific research assistant—a group you could easily find at a dinner party. But this group wanted to see if maybe it wasn't necessary to contact a preexisting spirit in a séance. They believed it might be possible to create their own.

And create they did. Meeting regularly, they imagined Philip Ayles-ford—a soul to whom they gave a birth date of 1624 and a death date of 1654, along with every imaginable type of specific detail of life. They dreamed up how he lived—as a soldier, as a knighted friend of the prince, and as a secret agent. They also dreamed up a tragic death, imagining how an affair with a Gypsy girl brought about an accusation of witchcraft against her from Philip's wife. After this girl was burned at the stake, Philip took his own life at the age of thirty. The group even drew pictures of what he looked like. The combined power of thought was at work. The authors comment on how the group became almost like a family, working well together and becoming rather tightly knit in time.

After months of meeting regularly to add reality to Philip, the group decided to contact him. Using one type of traditional séance, the eight sat around a table and got Philip to not only produce phantom raps and knocking, but they got their imagined friend to move the table as well. This was done in full light, in different rooms, and with different tables.

The noises and movements accomplished by Philip were his way of communicating answers to questions. A thinking thoughtform (although of limited intelligence), Philip truly believed himself to be the spirit that the group created him to be. He fed back in his own "words" messages containing the very facts that the group had decided upon earlier. Interestingly, he also embellished by providing authentic historical details from the 1600s (was this the group's subconscious at work?).

There's even an alleged documentary film that shows Philip manifesting. I'm still trying to get my hands on a copy of that, so I can't offer an opinion just yet, but experience has shown that phantom beings can be captured on video (see my book *Contact the Other Side*).

These examples of thoughtforms that influence the physical world are extreme. It's rarely necessary to create a phantom being, but it can be done.

Belief Barriers, Baffling Behavior

The group conjuring Philip began to believe in his existence and were certain that any phenomena experienced in a sitting would come from him. As these very beliefs grew in intensity, so did the phenomena. Likewise, David-Neel had experienced many mysteries in the East to put her in the right frame of mind to work with the monks who already believed in the possibility of thoughtform creation. In both the Toronto group and the combined efforts of the Tibetan monks, any belief barriers were shattered before thoughtforms became tangible.

What can you do to shatter yours? First you have to understand that it's a two-step process, because there are actually two types of barriers to mystical advancement: conscious and subconscious. These barriers can also be called "permanent" and temporary barriers, respectively.

Why quotation marks around the word "permanent"? Because your conscious barrier will only be there forever if you do nothing about it. You can make it go away. The conscious barrier you have now is the barrier or nagging voice that tells you: "This spiritual stuff can't work." You've likely already begun to take the first steps toward disabling it if you've done even one spell that worked. If so, you know firsthand that there's something to all this stuff. Keep practicing magick and Witchcraft, and in time your conscious barrier will not be so permanent at all. When such a time comes about, ritual psychodrama will be unnecessary. You will be able to merely will your request for change to make it come about.

Seem like a catch-22? Are you wondering how can you get any ritual successes if this conscious barrier exists? The confusion will disappear once you consider the more easily penetrated temporary or subconscious barrier. You can punch through this barrier with the use of psychodrama, thereby creating miracles with the power of the mind. Penetrate your subconscious barrier often enough, and your conscious barrier will no longer be able to affect you, either. It's really that simple.

Once again: Use ritual psychodrama to penetrate the temporary subconscious barrier and get results—the accumulated results will shatter your conscious barrier, taking away its permanence.

This simple secret, once mastered, opens up the mysteries of the universe to the practicing Witch. No need to read any more on theories about why this works. Put it into practice immediately, and be the one to tell others of its effectiveness.

The dissolution of your mental barriers is not the only thing you can do to boost all your magickal efforts, thoughtforms included. There is another bit of mental modification you may want to consider. Some of you may even be putting this into practice already.

Now, I'm expecting to receive some criticism for the next modification. If you're in on my way of thinking about what follows, terrific. If not, I hope you'll at least hear me out before deciding it's not for you.

One of the greatest aids to magick is attaining a childlike sense of wonder.

Not so controversial yet, right? Perhaps it's even something you've considered in passing. Fear not—we'll get to my suggestions that will raise more than a few eyebrows in a moment.

How to attain a childlike sense of wonder? I advise you to truly allow your mind and body some playtime, either in or out of a ritual setting. Some rituals contain elaborate pathworkings (guided visualizations) or roleplaying sessions to foster a creative, playful atmosphere before the real work begins. Sinking into somewhat childlike states was even done by the Toronto group in the Philip experiment, where before each session they would sing children's songs and behave in juvenile fashion for a short time.

Why this works is no real mystery. As children, our barriers are at their weakest and our imaginations are at their strongest. By seeking out childlike pleasures and states of mind, we create a sympathetic key that unlocks the magickal states of mind we were capable of in those preconditioning years of our development. The effects of the restrictive, physical world of adulthood don't seem to exist in these states, and can't adversely affect our magick.

Now, for the controversy.

I suggest that, whenever possible, you take joy in the pleasures of the night. Those who seek entertainment after dark experience altered states with little or no effort. Many of you know this to be true. I'm not recommending anything morally questionable; merely that you "play" in ways that darkness allows for, some examples of which follow.

If there's a music scene you're drawn to, spend some time in the clubs, listening to your favorite songs and observing the pulsing lights. Personally, I love Goth clubs, but I won't categorize those reading this. Dance freely, and allow your mounting elation to help you forget the rigid waking world. Play, in this fashion, whenever possible. (Incidentally, if you drink—at all—do not attempt any ritual work while under the influence. Such experiences will not be effective ones, as you need an unimpaired consciousness to achieve mystical change.)

So far, this doesn't sound too controversial, right? At least, it won't to many of you. But there will be some who consider clubbing and the like to be wastes of time; some who consider any kind of partying to be immature (although that's kind of the idea here!). To them we can say that magick after dark requires being attuned to the dark. Nocturnal Witchcraft requires nocturnal practitioners. There's a reason they're called *night*clubs, these places where we can revel till dawn (depending on your city). The part of you that takes pleasure in the smoke and flashing colored lights is a part you shouldn't repress. It may act as your link to just the right innocent state of mind required for ritual.

You can also tap this innocence without leaving home. Try getting together with friends at night and doing anything from watching movies into the wee hours to spending time just reliving exciting memories. Try to recall how much fun it was to defy bedtime while growing up. Having a slumber party of sorts, at any age, can awaken childlike wonder.

The point is, do not deprive yourself of the types of fun you wish to have after dark. As long as you're harming no one, including yourself, you just might be helping along your magickal causes by, for instance, dancing until last call.

Nocturnal Covens and Group Power

Many of us feel the need to be with like-minded individuals from time to time. In Witchcraft, we can get together for more than social purposes. Covens, throughout the decades, have been groups of Witches that celebrate the holidays together, help each other train, and combine efforts to accomplish magickal goals.

Groups are everywhere in the occult world, aren't they?

Not just limited to covens, magickal groups exist in every culture and mystical system. Rare is the spiritual path that demands solitary work. And even the types of shamans and medicine men who work alone seem to call on the aid of others, even if they are from the unseen world.

In the examples of thoughtforms discussed so far in this chapter, they were created by decent sized groups—as many as dozens in the case of Tibetan miracles, and eight in the Toronto Philip experiment.

Why all this teaming up? Surely it's not just for social needs.

Recall that magick is using your will to set a desirable chain of events in motion, or to change an undesirable chain that is in motion. Will is the key, and the more of it you have at your disposal the better. This is common sense, I suppose.

The more people there are building on a visualization in the astral plane, the stronger and better defined the form will be, and the quicker it will materialize on the physical plane.

What's not so obvious is that a group of two or three doesn't just double or triple the effectiveness of a rite. A person is much more than merely a battery to be tapped. When we have others lend their energy to a visualization and thoughtform, we are also allowing their own motivation and drive into our magick. Each person may want a particular result for slightly different reasons. Each of these reasons has different emotional driving factors behind it. And each of these emotionally charged motives adds a dimension of life to a thoughtform. The goal is to have a thoughtform that is free to act in as many ways as possible to accomplish a goal. Put simply, each person building on a visualization will see different potentials for the thoughtform, and the thoughtform will then have more potential ways of acting toward performing its function.

For example, a thoughtform designed to protect a home would not only be stronger when created by two people, but would also be able to act on both people's paranoia, if you will. While one Witch might be concerned with the thoughtform keeping others out, the second Witch might imagine fire and weather damage being averted.

In the case of Philip, having eight people build his form made it possible for each to clearly imagine some aspect of his appearance or past. The group was therefore better able to maintain its overall creativity, as no one person felt responsible for the entire form. It was built in unison, and lent strength in unison. However, if the group didn't get along, Philip would have likely never manifested.

Something to consider.

A magickal rite will only be strengthened by a group that is truly in unison. If there is dissonance among its members, a group will create a muddled, fuzzy thoughtform that at best will do nothing, and at worst will do the wrong thing. Be certain that those you choose to work with share your goals. Choose only to work with someone who understands and practices the same techniques you've mastered so far in this book.

The next section shows how all these preparations will enable you to bring your thoughtforms to startling, perhaps tangible, life.

Molding the Night

Whether you choose to work alone or with others, you will succeed at what follows. While the development of your receptive psychic skills and the accuracy of feats like mind reading may take years to finely hone, the act of creating mystical change in the universe can be mastered within weeks. And that's including the time it takes to succeed at the previous chapters' basic visualizing and skrying exercises.

If you can achieve even some degree of inner quiet, and if you can visualize at all—and I don't mean seeing cinema-quality visions—you can create a thoughtform. If you can skry, you will be able to monitor your thoughtform's effectiveness—a practice I stumbled upon quite accidentally, as I'll share later.

What can you expect from the thoughtforms you create? Know that Witchcraft is practical. Whether you're concerned with an immediate need or the theurgic desire to perfect yourself over time, you should be interested in using the Nocturnal Craft to attain results. And that's what you can expect: results.

The thoughtforms you'll be working with in this book are not intended for show. They are not the stuff of party games, and shouldn't be used to create solid object as did the Tibetan monks, or poltergeist-like phenomena as did the Philip group. Using the technique you're about to learn, you will be able to create change that will physically manifest in time. Here the process is providing for a successful end—it is not the end itself. If you only want to learn how to make thoughtforms that you can touch and show off, you're not practicing Witchcraft.

But still, the mentioned examples of thinking and independently acting thoughtforms given so far are not entirely out of context. Using an advanced technique you'll learn in the *Gothic Grimoire*, you'll be able to create a nocturnal servant that can be assigned whatever task you wish (again, Witchcraft is about getting results). Depending on how it's created, and by how many Witches, one of these servants may just become visible and tangible. Depending on the task you have assigned for it, a solid servant might be shockingly effective at carrying out its duties. I can imagine a solid thoughtform would handle something like protection in unforgettable ways!

Even as they work in unseen ways for you, however, the thoughtforms you are about to master here should never be underestimated. I can't stress enough that, once mastered, the technique that follows will make you feel as if you have at your disposal an unlimited number of genie-granted wishes.

To create this type of thoughtform, you will need to decide on a need, of course. You will also need to choose a God or Goddess that is related to the need. The reason for this is because thoughtforms should be created in a full circle, with either a simple invocation or full god-form assumption (your choice per ritual). For either form of invocation, you will have to work with the "right" deity. We've gone into this selection process already, and you should be comfortable consulting appendix A or looking at various books on mythology to find the right nocturnal God or Goddess—to find a deity that seems to be associated with the task you are trying to accomplish.

With magickal need and deity name decided upon, go on to write a spell using the following structure:

Begin your spell with a line that reiterates the reason you are calling a particular God or Goddess on this night. Follow this with as many lines in the body of the spell as it takes to get across your magickal need. Next, explain in one line that the spell is working to create a thoughtform—do so by saying something like: "I will into being this request, my thoughts shall physically manifest." Add a line now that condenses your statements of desire into a mantra, just as you did with the dream rite in the previous chapter (remember to try and word this statement as if you have already achieved the goal). Close the written spell with your "harm none" line of choice.

Set up your altar and room for ritual, then place your written spell face down in front of the nocturnal portal.

Note that like all techniques in this book, the following one is written for solitary use. If you wish to create a thoughtform with the help of another person, be sure to begin your collaboration by taking turns doing parts of the circle casting. Then, one of you should take charge, performing the invocation and reading the spell. Both participants can perform the visualization described in the rite, as well as the energy raising done.

Thoughtform Creation

Cast the nocturnal circle through step twenty-five.

Meditate for a moment on how the nocturnal portal is reflecting the tangible substance of night that exists right outside your circle.

Pick up the spell with your receiving hand.

Hold your open projecting hand a couple of inches away from the surface of the nocturnal portal. Your palm and extended fingers should be parallel to the skrying tool.

Become aware of the glow or "lighter darkness" inside the portal. See your hand's reflection in there, and feel the dark glow as a tingling on your hand.

Look away from the mirror, close your eyes, and raise some emotional energy (about half of what you'd normally do for a ritual).

Open your eyes and read the spell, allowing your emotional energy to peak (at a reduced level) as you read the mantra line.

Finish the words and look at the portal. Lower your hand slightly until its reflection just disappears.

Repeat the mantra and concentrate on the glow in the portal. Begin to see the portal as the large, glowing sphere of nocturnal energy that it has become.

Still repeating the mantra, try to visualize yourself, within the glowing portal, as having achieved whatever it is you're asking for. This image will most likely resemble the fulfilled words of your mantra, but if some other strong image comes to you, see it clearly instead.

You are visualizing not in the portal now, but in an energy sphere that is cohabiting the same space as your portal. Know this to be true. Sense that the glowing sphere is its own "thing."

Still repeating the mantra and visualizing within the portal, begin to raise emotional energy again. This time, you will be trying to reach your maximum energy level.

When you feel the energy about to peak, put all your muscles into the release. Thrust your projecting palm toward the portal (without making contact). Shout the mantra one last time. And, as all this happens, see the glowing sphere that has inhabited the mirror, the glowing sphere that still contains your visualized image, blast away from you, up the angle of the portal. See this glowing sphere clearly launch off toward the east, out of your circle, and into night.

Drop to the floor, close your eyes, and concentrate on feeling how tangible the circle around you is. Do not look at the portal or altar again for a minute or so.

Stand up and close your circle from step twenty-seven on.

Try not to think about the thoughtform again this night.

Checking Up on Thoughtforms

As simple as it may seem, the preceding technique—a culmination of the techniques you've been learning a chapter at a time—will achieve dazzling results. You can be certain of this, and will see what I mean when your thoughtform does its job. However, I can't be there to reassure you of your success if you have to wait a few days for said results.

I can let you in on something that helps me pass time when I'm waiting for my magick to work, though.

How nice it would be to be able to say that I came up with this technique in a vision or through some translation of an ancient manuscript. But, like so many discoveries, this one was a pure accident.

I had just performed a thoughtform to help a friend. Two days passed, and nothing in her situation had changed. Her distress about this important rite (for her) was making me anxious. Because of her lack of faith, I was losing faith—not a good thing. Keep this in mind: Thinking negatively about a thoughtform creates another thoughtform to counteract your original one. This is the reason you should always keep your magickal workings to yourself, at least until the results manifest.

There I was, probably beginning to coalesce thoughts against my original magick. I started to cast a circle to just bask in the elation of invocation—I needed a pick-me-up to counter the low spirits that had rubbed off on me. But I never got to the invocation. When I looked at my portal to trace the spirit pentagram, I got a flash of how the thought-form would manifest. It was a vision of my friend agreeing to an experimental bit of surgery that might correct her problem. Sure enough, this surgery was offered in a few days and was successful.

Rather than let yourself sink into doubt, feel free to ask the night how your thoughtform is coming along in its manifestation of your desire. Do not ask *if* it is succeeding—ask only how far along it is toward succeeding.

A properly created thoughtform, as well as properly performed magick of any type, always works.

Voice this query in a cast circle and before your nocturnal portal. Then see the path your magick will take to fulfilling your dreams.

You know how to do this.

Chapter Twelve

Dark Mystique, Magnetism, and Suggestion

The world is not always a kind place for those who are different . . . unless they are liked, of course.

As one of nightkind, you move through the world as a member of a minority soul-type. Likely misunderstood and occasionally even feared, you must find ways to either let others in on what makes you different, or deal with possible harsh treatment from those who don't understand.

We're far removed from the Burning Times, of course, but being a Witch is still not the easiest thing to be open about. There will come times when you are made uncomfortable by the negative attentions of those who either don't quite get what you are, or who get it but don't quite agree with what you practice.

Revealed here are some secrets that adepts, both light and dark, have used to make it easier to "get by" while being different. Essentially, they're the secrets of personal magnetism and mystique, of creating a variety of perceptions in the minds of those around you—perceptions that can help you peacefully coexist with the owners of said minds. Practiced in the way taught here, the techniques you're about to learn pose no danger to your karma or to the welfare of any. This is not mind control!

Rather, to ensure peace in your life, you'll find that certain kinds of attentions are best not attracted, while certain reverences from others are desirable. Achieving these magickal modifications to your social surroundings is what this chapter's all about.

Your Dark Mystique

Dark mystique is what you make of it. As we briefly touched on in the previous chapter, it is important to keep silent about your magickal workings to prevent others from creating negative thoughtforms that can work against the thoughtforms you create in ritual. Yet it is also helpful to keep silent about what you do in your magickal life overall. Besides creating an air of mystery about you, such silence can prevent others from sending adverse thoughts about your chosen path.

Not everyone in your daily contact need know everything about you. They may know you are a Witch, but may know little more, making you a mysterious figure indeed. The less they know, the less they can counteract.

Of course, people tend to fear what they don't understand, and you don't want to draw that kind of negative attention. You'll want to let out just enough information to sate the curiosity around you, and at the same time maintain silence about the important things.

Don't let others have power over you with their thoughts!

Deciding what to tell others is something you'll have to determine on a case-by-case basis. All I can recommend is that you err on the side of secrecy. Offer information sparingly, and watch your personal store of power build. Again, your thoughtforms and spells will work better when they can act uninhibited.

If you're ever not certain just how much of your mystique to dispel to any given person, listen to the night or perform a simple mind reading of the person. If you get even the slightest indication that maybe you should remain silent about a part of what it is you do, then listen to instinct. Trust your developing abilities on this.

And, as you might have read in other Witchcraft books, we don't proselytize. Don't feel a need to convert the world by talking about how wondrous your powers and religion are. Those who are ready for the Craft, nocturnal or more traditional, will find it on their own. The Gods work in mysterious ways, indeed.

Let your own happiness and feeling of security rule what you reveal to others.

The Magnetism Surrounding You

Not everyone fears nightkind. Some find the so-called children of the night to be anything from quirky to alluring and beautiful. And all outsiders find something noticeable about the dark ones, don't they?

They pick up on your dark magnetism—a simple yet powerful aspect of your nature that can make it easier to get by in numerous situations.

As most people are tuned to the light, we nightkind stand out. Chances are that you've felt this to be so even when you've dressed in the most conservative ways. If it's not just the clothes or makeup, what can it be?

Night's energies are tangible, as you've found by now. This moldable energy tends to sympathetically follow you. Even in daylight, you'll find you can somewhat raise up the special feeling you get when in a nocturnal circle at night. Unlike some movie creature, your connection to your power does not disappear when the sun comes up. Your aura will always reveal, even to those without developed astral senses, your dark and powerful nature.

Your personal nature made manifest in your aura is part of your dark magnetism. As you practice night's mysteries, this nocturnal presence will only increase in intensity, having a magnetic effect on others.

No extra effort is required in this respect. Develop your dark mystical abilities and magnetism will follow. The energy around you will not be ignored!

But, being a fan of mystical shortcuts, I've come up with a simple way to boost the potency of your aura's magnetism. It's a little trick to getting your auric energy to affect others quickly.

Ten Seconds to Magnetism

Try, whenever possible, to have great deliberation in movements and actions.

Imagine, from time to time, that something even as simple as opening a door requires magickal willpower in addition to the ordinary physical movement involved. When you decide on such a course of action, gaze at the selected object for a moment, imagining yourself doing the action.

Raise some emotional energy, and perform the action quickly and with severity.

Any time you act in such a way, your aura will give off extra vibes that others will pick up on. Try it and see.

Not only will such deliberate actions have a magnetic effect on others, but they will also provide practical reasons to practice and improve your ability to raise emotional energy on demand. As you've seen, this energy is useful for most everything in Witchcraft.

Casting Illusions

Mystique and magnetism make others feel that there is something indefinable about you. It is also possible, however, to make others sense that there is something specific and amazing about you. The power that makes it possible is illusion.

Now, let's be clear about what I mean by illusion. Only the most powerful of adepts can make others see what he or she wants them to.

The illusion we'll deal with is a more subtle type that you can put into use right away.

We're not talking about creating thoughtforms to fool others into thinking that there's a brick wall in their path or to make people see other types of flashy phenomena. Rather, the practice taught here makes it possible to alter your aura to create the unseen impression that things around you are not quite what they seem.

You can use illusion to make yourself more approachable—say, when preparing for an important event. Or, alternatively, you can use the art to make yourself seem as if you are not worth approaching by aggressors—say, when walking home from an important event at three in the morning.

The technique for doing so is very simple, building on your ability to work with thoughtforms. As with all mental magick, it gets much stronger with time and practice, so work on this whenever you can.

The Illusory Aura

Decide on the sensation or perception that you want others to have of you.

Turn the desired sensation into a positive, present-tense mantra (for example, "Those who wish me harm must turn away").

Close your eyes and imagine that your aura is silver. It reaches out approximately a foot and a half in every direction.

Begin to repeat your mantra while imagining your aura morphing into a shape related to your wish. For protection rites, imagine scales or something similar. For attracting others, imagine that your aura is dazzling and beautiful. For subtle invisibility, imagine that a dark cloak is materializing around your aura. The possibilities are limited only by your visualization and imagination.

When you've designed and created a visual symbol that gets across the illusion you want to portray, begin to raise emotional energy. You should still be repeating the mantra.

See the changes to your aura as clearly as possible and peak your emotional energy to charge the image. If possible, shout the mantra out loud one last time at the peak.

Now you can walk about as normal with your illusion blanketing you. Reinforce your illusion by imagining, from time to time, that you actually look like the visual symbol you imagined.

When you have no further need for the illusion, imagine the form of your aura dissolving back to a uniform silver field. Then, perform a banishing to ensure that this is so.

Planting Suggestions

More active than illusion, suggestion makes it possible to send subtle yet specific commands to others. Now, we're no longer speaking of the power of suggestion. Rather, mystical suggestion—a technique where you use energy to transmit ideas.

Note that these simple techniques will never cause someone to act against his or her will. As mentioned earlier, the techniques taught in this chapter are not mind control by any means. Rather, suggestion helps nudge others into possible courses of action that are for the greater good of all . . . as well as harmonious to your own will.

Before you try to plant a suggestion, listen to the night for inspiration on what you are about to do. Ask if your suggestion will truly be for the greater good. If you get any negative feeling or sense that you're treading dangerous territory, do not proceed.

A good time to consider using suggestion is whenever you feel you are about to enter a hostile situation and could use a quick edge in your favor. You may suggest in such a situation that a particular person either "lighten up" with respect to his or her attitude toward you, or that he or she look the other way when it comes to some of your activities.

You may also want to use suggestion if you're simply trying to get someone's attention. I don't mean you should use it to try to enslave someone—this would have heavy karmic consequences, undoubtedly.

You can use suggestion, however, as you would use a stunning outfit or flashy conversation piece. Let suggestion be the little something extra that draws someone to your vicinity, and let your own personality and magnetism do the rest.

Simple suggestions can be sent in two ways that we'll get to presently. The first should obviously be done at night—during psychic quiet time, actually. The second can be done whenever, although you know by now that nighttime is best.

Influencing the Dreaming

Obtain a picture or personal item of the person to whom you're attempting to impart a suggestion. If this fails, try to come up with some item that at least reminds you of the person. In an absolute pinch, his or her name written on a piece of paper will have to do.

Decide on a simple suggestion, phrased in the present tense. The suggestion should do just that—suggest a possibility. Something like, "Think of me for the open assistant manager position" is ideal. Do not try to force an action with a statement like, "You will give me the open assistant manager position."

Between the hours of 3 and 5 A.M., do a banishing and begin to achieve some inner quiet.

By candlelight, focus on the picture or object you chose. Try to imagine the person clearly with your open eyes. This will be easier if you're using a photograph, but either way try to imagine that the person is superimposed over the photo or object. Imagine that he or she is about a foot tall, and floating over the item as a phantom. See this person as having his or her eyes closed.

Meditate for a moment on the fact that you are observing this person asleep. Try to let the visualization become as solid as possible in the air before you. If the image becomes so real to you that you can't see the object behind it, all the better.

Sense a glowing silver sphere inside your throat, but do so without taking away any strength from the visualization before you.

State your suggestion out loud and feel the words vibrate in your throat. The sphere is absorbing these words . . . do you feel it?

Raise some emotional energy and feel the sphere pulse even more in your throat.

When you're about halfway to peaking with emotional energy, repeat the phrase. Do not take your eyes off the visualized form before you.

Repeat the phrase once more just as you're about to peak. When this energy level is finally reached, blast the sphere out of your throat, through your neck, and into the visualized form before you.

Let your open eyes bulge open even wider, in a fierce gaze at the floating form.

Repeat the phrase once more and immediately blow out the candle. Leave the room for a few minutes.

Your suggestion will enter the mind of this person through his or her dreams.

The bulging of the eyes in the preceding (and following) technique helps you to transmit all the energy in your body related to the thoughtform. It also acts as a physiological trigger to releasing you of the mental state you drifted into while doing the rite.

Now, for those times when you're in the room with the person you want to send a suggestion to. . . .

Suggestions to the Waking

Find a spot from where you can see the person to whom you wish to make a suggestion. You should be close enough to have no major obstacles in your path, but far enough so that he or she doesn't notice you. This person can have his or her back to you, and this is even recommended, as you'll be staring at this person for a few moments.

Decide on a simple suggestion phrase, following the same guidelines given in the preceding dream-contact technique.

Try to achieve some inner quiet in this place, which is likely to be public.

Imagine a glowing silver sphere inside your forehead or third eye area.

State your suggestion phrase in a whisper, or to yourself if someone is close by. Try to feel these low or imagined words vibrating the sphere in your forehead.

Raise some emotional energy and feel the sphere pulse even more, seeming to almost bulge out of your brow.

About halfway to peaking, whisper or silently repeat the phrase. Be sure to maintain a view of the person.

Just as you're about to peak, repeat the phrase once more. Fire the sphere out of your forehead when you peak, sending it into the head of the person.

Open your eyes wider in the most fierce gaze you can get away with in public.

Repeat the phrase, and leave the area for a couple of minutes.

When you next come into range of the person, consider some kind of dramatic way to come into his or her view. Think along the lines of what was discussed in the practice of mind dowsing in chapter 8. In other words, supplement your mystical suggestion with the power of visual or verbal suggestion.

Seen dramatically by the person, you will only reinforce the fact that you're currently on his or her mind. If you're feeling particularly daring, you can even say something that will reinforce what you tried to make the person think of. But do not repeat the phrase you mentally sent. Try something that contains one or two of the same words, or a phrase that somehow relates to the topic of the mystical suggestion.

With the ability to both create change in this world and move among its masses with greater ease, your life will be enhanced by orders of magnitude. I suppose we could end this book here.

But there is one other world worth attaining some mastery over.

And one more powerful being I think it's important for you to meet.

Chapter Thirteen

Death: His/Her Mysteries

Is there really a Death with a capital D? Does an entity or godform guide the process of our departure from this world? Tallying up a list of the cultures that have believed this to be so would be much more difficult than listing those that didn't. But is Death, the being, a silly primitive notion, or something based in occult fact?

And, entity embodying the state or not, what is death? What happens to us *after*? Further, if souls survive the great ripping out from the flesh, can they be contacted?

It's a loaded chapter that will hopefully answer some of these questions, and provide you with the keys you'll need to answer the rest for yourself.

An Anthropomorphic Death

We neopagans give names and faces to our Gods. As we explored in chapter 3, seeing the Creator as anthropomorphic, or humanlike, provides us with an easier way of connecting with particular aspects of its primal, overwhelming energy. In Nocturnal Witchcraft, the God and Goddess forms we give Divinity group nicely into six categories. We've looked so far at five of the types: the deities of Night Personified, the Dark Moon, the Full Moon, Protection, and Descent and Rebirth.

Now, for the legendary Gods of the Underworld.

If we feel comfortable accessing the Source through names associated with specific energies, then it's not so strange to think of death as having deities or beings attributed to it. What force or aspect of creation has more impact on our lives, after all? If we can attribute God names to love, protection, and other currents that affect each of our nights, then why can't we identify the Gods and Goddesses of the Underworld?

Right off, I should note that my beliefs surrounding the afterlife hardly justify my calling this realm the Underworld. I've only referred to Death personified as coming from the Underworld because that is how the ancients saw the afterlife, and using the terminology helps to classify the Gods of Death found in myth.

The Death we'll be speaking of comes from a much nicer place, as it turns out. But we'll get to the "where" later, and stick to the "who" for now.

Assuming for a moment that he or she exists (you'll decide for yourself later on), who would this dark one be? Besides being just another face of the Source, Death would have to be a hard-working manifestation indeed. Every soul that passed on from this existence would have to be embraced and carried away by such a one as Death. Hovering within various emotional settings of sorrow and shock on earth, Death would have to take newly disembodied souls and clear away the confusion, bringing the souls hope. He or she would have to be the one to let them know what awaits them, and show them the way to reach it.

Does this idea of cosmic duty sound odd? It didn't and doesn't to me, after working with ritual magick. As I relate in *Summoning Spirits*,

Gods and Goddesses are not the only anthropomorphic or personified versions of universal energies. The angels and demons of ancient grimoires, along with countless other entities found in these books of conjuring, are beings with distinct personalities and attributes and are assigned, if you will, to offices or posts in the universe.

I believed in the possibility of a Death personified because of the existence of these other assigned or allocated occult beings.

I now believe in the fact that Death exists, having met him or her . . . or it.

Recall my description in chapter 3 of Ereshkigal and the force she emitted? There I mentioned that it wasn't the first time I had felt this type of presence.

The first time I met the entity Death—in the early 1990s—I was not performing any kind of ritual. I was beginning a routine, thirty-minute drive home, yet something didn't feel quite routine that night.

I was a bit numb as I entered my car, almost as if I were only observing myself going through the motions of unlocking the door, getting behind the wheel, inserting the key in the ignition. I barely felt my flesh performing all these actions, and the feeling of detachment would only get worse.

In time the numbness became absolute. I began to feel as if I were a guest in my body, observing through someone else's eyes as the world rushed past me. The only tangible thing I did sense was the close proximity of that force-field-like weight I described earlier. It was in the passenger seat.

I couldn't turn my head to look—could only peripherally sense the presence. It seemed to have a form, if a vague, amorphous one. The darkness seemed to congeal and lighten, forming something like a black oval with a glowing center.

And strange thoughts began to enter my mind, thoughts seemingly broadcast from this being. As I felt my consciousness sinking farther into the background and my body acting more automatically, I began to think about how it was okay to truly let go. Not just of my actions this night, but of everything.

The numbness, I was being "told," was but an example of how there would be no pain. Of how easy death would be—yes, I sensed the word "death" in thought.

I was coming to a point in my trip where I could take one of two major roads home: either a parkway or a highway. I saw, now through an increasing blurriness of vision, my hands turning the wheel slightly. Apparently, I was about to merge onto the ramp for the highway. As my car edged onto the deserted ramp, I felt something like love, something like elation.

I knew this could be it. Could be, but didn't have to be. Does that make sense? Death didn't seem to be taking me with itself, he or she just seemed to be showing me that the option was there. Call it a warning or an offer, what this genderless being was providing. But I knew that if I let my car get onto the highway, Death would be fulfilling its duty.

When I came to this realization of what the road choice would mean, and that it was very much a choice, the numbness disappeared. I found myself in complete control of my body again.

As I pulled the wheel to the left (the road was deserted) to continue onto the parkway instead, I quickly glanced at the passenger seat. I saw something in the center of the fading darkness, but I can't share here what it was, this personal vision.

I was, and still am, very grateful that Death made itself known to me. It wasn't my time, and the visit wasn't meant as a threat. Rather, I like to think of it as a reminder of how close we come daily to the other side, and of how maybe there's some mechanism in place for making our transition less difficult.

Yes, I believe there is a Death with a capital *D*. I've met it in genderless form. I've met it as the Goddess Ereshkigal. Later, I would meet it as the God Anubis.

You're welcome to do the same.

Some of you might be asking "why" right about now. Why would anyone want to meet Death before his or her time has come? This doesn't exactly seem like a manifestation of Divine that the living have much reason to identify with.

Yet only Death can provide us with certain knowledge and reassurances. By accepting the reality of something more on the other side, we are free to continue on our magickal paths undaunted by the threat of it all being for naught. Also, by breaking down the belief barriers we have about an afterlife, we are free to contact those who are no longer with us.

Before we get to the idea of communing with Death the being, however, a little more on the process of what happens at death. What is this afterlife state all about?

What Happens When We Die?

In *Contact the Other Side*, which was in part assembled from messages delivered by the deceased, I go into great detail describing some of the sources for what follows in this section. However, some of the information disseminated in the aforementioned book and in this one comes from Death as well. I couldn't flag any information in *Contact the Other Side* as having come from Death, of course. This godform didn't really fit into a book designed for people of all religions, even if its message did, so I blended in the complementary information where I could.

How you, too, can get inspiration from Death will be explored in the next section.

But first, a condensed description of what happens when we die to put the afterlife into perspective. Remember, we're all here for a purpose, and all have a path to follow, nocturnal or not. Knowing something about the planes we move through after death—about how our souls spend parts of eternity—helps keep us on track; helps remind us, if you will, that our advancing souls are working toward something in the hereafter. As mentioned in chapter I, before we come to earth for an incarnation, we decide which lessons and experiences we need to have. Some of this is to make up for karma, some to expand our inner dimensions of being.

But before we can come back to earth, we depart.

When physical life ceases, our astral bodies leave the mortal shell. The astral body is what you access during an out-of-body experience in life, and is what you awaken a link to every time you raise up emotional energy. You can think of this body as being animated by lifeforce or energy that coexists, on the astral level, with the physical energy our life processes carry out. Without life, however, lifeforce soon burns out.

After our astral bodies leave their physical energy source, we become aware of moving away from our physical forms. If death is temporary, as when resuscitation is successful in a hospital, we'll be pulled back into the flesh and remember seeing ourselves on a hospital bed, and maybe remember more, which we'll get to. But if it really is time to move on, our astral bodies will linger in the astral plane, near the living, for a few hours or maybe a day or two. We then experience the second death, when our astral bodies run out of energy and disintegrate.

The second death, in my opinion, is when Death can actually do his or her job.

This astral end is not the end of our consciousness or that part of us most closely tied to the mental plane. Our consciousness, mental body, or soul, as most call it, leaves the astral body at the second death, much like our astral form left the flesh at physical death.

The universe guides the released soul, through the force of Death. Whether or not the soul sees Death depends likely on whether the person is open to the concept of anthropomorphic deities.

Actually, this is a good time to note something that is rarely if ever brought up on the topic of afterlife processes: As inspirational as they may be, the sights and sounds of near-death experiences (NDEs) can't be taken into account when determining what actual death is like.

Quite simply, during these visions, the second death hasn't happened yet, making a NDE a different set of circumstances than true death. Read a few descriptions of NDEs and you'll find that in almost every one the person sees loved ones . . . who seem to know the person's soul is going back into the body.

When a person is actually going to complete the process of death, they likely see something different. Souls from the other side who have relayed to me in messages what it's like to move on have never claimed to see loved ones until a bit later in the process, after the second death.

Death, the aspect of Divinity that controls the universal process involved in dying, guides the soul after it is freed from the astral body. This means that if you see Death while still alive, he or she probably isn't coming for you! The only time you can experience contact with Death and live to tell about it is while still in the flesh.

Now, back to what happens to a freed soul. With the help of Death or the universe's guiding energy, it moves on to the afterlife, a world of spiritual levels or realms. Just how far it goes or high it rises within the afterlife, however, depends on the soul's current stage of development.

The first level that the disincarnated soul enters, the low realm, is where lingering fascinations or even obsessions are worked out to purify the soul for further advancement. This kind of leftover baggage from life needs to be faced in a place that vibrates at a low frequency similar to the one we all experience during life. The low realm is therefore close to earth in many ways, and for this reason feels oppressive. It holds souls who are not ready to move on.

Nothing like the Christian concept of Hell, the low realm is not a place where souls are sentenced. It's just where one remains until he or she has worked out whatever major flaws prevent even reincarnation from taking place. Not everyone who dies will go to the low realm. Some souls accomplish enough good in their lives to be instantly drawn to higher realms than this, and will barely notice the low realm as they rocket up through it. The majority of good-dark or good-light individuals usually only have to spend brief amounts of time, if any, working out a few points in the low realm.

But some souls have failed, maybe even horribly, at their life goals. These who have so fallen to either evil-dark or evil-light soul types have a lot to work out. The low realm is where this learning and atonement occur. Evildoers will have to face dreamlike reenactments of their crimes against others and themselves, until their souls learn enough to move on. The realm reacts to the soul's state of mind and will only let the individual move on after he or she has learned all necessary lessons.

Death, the being, has no hand in the low realm's "management" or actual learning process. The personification of Death would only assist in making sure the soul makes the transition to the low realm. The realm takes over from there.

Think of Death as being a gatekeeper. The ancients didn't quite have it right when they referred to Death as being a sort of Lord or Lady of the Underworld. This misconception could have arisen from one of two types of experiences:

For one, people from ancient times could have had NDEs where Death met them at the brink of the second death, yet they came back. Were you to get close to the low realm, you would feel how much like an "underworld" it really is. But Death does not rule this place. He or she merely helps you enter.

Another way the Underworld Ruler title could have come around is through visionary work or skrying. An ancient mystic contacting a personification of Death (as you will soon do, if you wish), might have sensed that Death lurks between here and the low realm. Sensing the proximity of Death to the oppressive low realm, a skryer might have misinterpreted this Underworld as being the final destination of a soul.

But remember, Death is not a fearsome denizen of some abysmal place. He or she is another aspect of Divinity, and one that is helpful to our spiritual growth.

Back to the low realm, now. If a soul is kept there by its low vibrations or lack of advancement, it receives a life review. It is made aware of any fixations and addictions that have to be resolved, and experiences other dramas that got it there. A definite way to end up in the low realm is through suicide. This universal crime has a heavy karmic debt, and some of it must be paid off by first grasping why it's horrible to give up on your life's purpose. Souls will see what could have been, and reenact what went wrong, until they are freed of some of the karma.

But suicides and even criminals can move on. The afterlife is a place seeking balance, and only uses the low realm to prepare souls for transitioning to higher levels.

The first of these higher levels is the summer realm, often referred to by Witches as the Summerland. Resembling earth on pleasant nights and sunny days, this is where most disincarnated souls reside. Thought is both power and reality here, and the dead can create their own surroundings, from homes to physical appearances. Talk about powerful magick! Anything you will in the Summerland instantly manifests.

Like-minded individuals congregate here, resulting in groups of souls with similar religious beliefs getting together. But souls can interact with any deceased whom they come across, and even enjoy a kind of social life, complete with etheric hangouts and entertainment.

You can read more about life on the other side in my aforementioned book on the subject. But for now, just keep in mind that it's not such a bad existence. Nor is it one without purpose.

The Summerland, in particular, is a microcosmic version of our purpose for being. Here we continue to experience new things, dark and light, becoming more advanced beings that are closer to the Source. Yet it's still not possible to learn all the universe's lessons in the Summerland, where thought creates reality. To really struggle or strive for anything, we need to be on the physical plane, where things don't come so easy and physical laws limit the impact our mental powers have on our surroundings. We can still do magick, but it's more restrictive on earth than in the Summerland. Time spent on the physical plane helps us advance faster, therefore, as we truly have to work through many problems.

Souls decide in the Summerland when to reincarnate to help their development. They choose which lessons to experience, and are drawn to a fertilized egg on earth that will be born into an appropriate life situation. I guess I needed to be a 6'6" male occult author and Goth vocalist in this incarnation, but could just as easily have chosen a 5'2" female dressmaker in another life. Either way, I know I'd still be a Witch!

Again, as mentioned in chapter I, you chose this incarnation you're living.

Eventually, you will choose not to incarnate at all. One day, you'll have learned all your lessons and be ready to reunite with the Source—ready to be with the God and Goddess in purest form, both theirs and yours.

Such reunion with that font that created us occurs in a higher, more spiritual realm, where we no longer feel the need to create earthlike appearances or surroundings. But as for any more information about this realm, it's not too easily attained.

As I've found in my afterlife communication experiments, few souls from the spiritual realms communicate with the living. Clear communication with the living is only possible from souls in the Summerland. Souls from higher realms have to come down to the Summerland's middle ground to communicate with us.

An important note here: A soul can come down to lower realms at will, but cannot rise higher than its level of advancement. Those in the low realm, for instance, cannot rise up to the Summerland, say for the purpose of making clear contact with the living. There are times when souls in the low realm manage to communicate with the living, but they do so from said land of confusion, resulting in confused, somewhat disturbing messages. Many hauntings are impressions we receive of souls in the low realm that still have connections to specific physical places. As the low realm is only a "hair" away from the physical world, the souls working through issues in the low realm do from time to time make themselves known to us in specific, haunted places.

Back to our discussion of higher realms, however. Neither I nor other occultists involved with afterlife research have received many messages from those in the higher realms who have become so far separated from human ways of being and thinking. Some common ideas come across from these advanced souls, however. Here's what I've found, if you care to hear my summation: There comes a point where the Source makes itself known to us in its universal form. At this moment we'll understand how the Source truly does encompass everything, and we'll be ready to reunite with it. As for what that must be like, I couldn't even guess.

Before we leave the subject of our development, let me add that those of us open to the idea of a God and Goddess are already open to the universality of the Source. Next time you're stressing about finding just the right deity name, remember that these links all really do go to the same place—a place we have an eventual appointment with.

Why You'd Want to Meet Him or Her

As you can see, the afterlife is not a realm ruled by Death. Rather, he or she is the gatekeeper to such a realm. And even if you don't believe in the necessity for such a being, you can still accept that there must be an aspect of Divinity that controls the process. Call that Death, or something else if you need to, but there is something controlling how our souls enter the afterlife.

Would you like to speak with this part of Divinity?

We already said that you should not invoke Underworld deities—Death godforms—for just any magickal rite. These beings can only help with contacting the dead or getting more information about the afterlife. Okay, maybe "can only help" isn't doing these Gods and Goddesses justice! No small feats, these aforementioned ones.

While we won't go into all the possible nuances of afterlife communication here, the special Death godform assumption technique you're about to learn will make it possible to contact the dead in one magickal way.

Before you attempt to speak with a lost loved one, however, there is a lot to consider. Most important is the need to determine what you expect from afterlife communication. The dead cannot be part of our daily life, for instance, nor do they have all the answers to our problems. If you have a strong need to connect again with someone now on the other side, you really should make sure you straighten all your expectations out beforehand. This is all handled in *Contact the Other Side*, along with non-magickal techniques for communication. At least try to borrow a copy of that book if all you wish to do is check out some of the emotional preparation steps that are out of the scope of the book you're now reading.

Until you're certain you know why you wish to speak with a certain deceased being, however, you can still proceed with the assumption of Death's form. The experience can be used, as I mentioned, to learn more about the afterlife. Knowledge of our destination after death will help you accept reincarnation and the idea that you're here to elevate your consciousness, and will help you succeed at your goals.

It doesn't make sense to be a Witch and believe it all ends with death. You would never truly unlock your abilities to create change in the world and your life if you maintained such a pessimistic outlook. And it's more than just your mood at stake, here. The afterlife is not a fantasy to keep us happy while alive. It is a reality, and all occultists should be aware of what makes up reality.

Ready to obtain the proof of all this? Ready to speak with Death and, even, the dead?

I can't recommend what you should try to accomplish in your dialogue with Death. If, by now, you have no desire to interact with this figure—this being who holds so many answers to the questions or insecurities you may have had—perhaps you're not ready for the dialogue. That's fine. There's a lot of magick to be done, and a lot of other aspects of Nocturnal Divinity to make contact with.

But if you do feel the need, success is not far away. You've already learned everything necessary to physically and mystically accomplish a dialogue with Death. In the *Gothic Grimoire* we'll be going into the Underworld threshold rite I described in chapter I. This will be presented in context with some other things you'll need to know to make it work.

For now, we'll be looking at another ancient paradigm for communicating with Death.

A Dialogue with Death and the Dead

In the ancient Leyden Papyrus (see Suggested Reading), there are numerous visionary rites where deities, including Anubis, reveal mysteries to the skryer. This gave me the idea to develop the following rite for working with Anubis, the Egyptian gatekeeper to the afterlife. You can certainly substitute another God or Goddess for Anubis with modifications to the words and correspondences mentioned, but do look into Anubis before you do so. His godform is one that has built up a lot of potency over the millennia, and you might want to make his acquaintance in your quest for dark knowledge.

The rite is designed to allow you to know bits of what Anubis knows, see flashes of what he sees in the Underworld or afterlife. In many ways, what follows is a typical godform assumption, with time devoted to receiving visions that the God grants. Yet the ritual adds a step that will even enable you to call forth a particular deceased individual. You can skip this part, however, if you only wish to be in Anubis's presence.

To perform the rite, you will need a fully set up altar. The Nocturnal Portal will play an important role in what you are about to undertake, as will your ability at skrying.

If you will be trying to contact a deceased loved one, try to obtain some personal item of his or hers. This can be anything that you can easily hold in one hand. A photo can be used, but would be more effective if it was a personal photo that the deceased person actually owned at one point. The personal item should be placed somewhere on top of your altar to the side that corresponds to your receiving hand. In other words, if you're standing facing east, with the altar before you, the object should be to the side of your receiving hand. Or you can lean the object up against that side if it's too large to fit on top of the altar.

For this rite, try to burn kyphi, a blended Egyptian incense you can buy or make yourself. Myrrh or sandalwood will also work, however. You can place a statue or picture of Anubis on your altar if you wish—the popularity of the Egyptian pantheon makes it possible to find reasonably priced statuary. Anubis looks pretty much the same in most art, except for one important distinction: he can be either in the form of a man with a jackal head, or in full jackal form. It's okay to have either representation on the altar, but do not try to assume the full jackal form! Only assume the human godform with jackal head.

While the statue or picture is optional, there is one important representation of Anubis that should not be omitted from the rite: an ankh.

A three-dimensional ankh that you can pick up and hold (not a picture) is a necessity. A small pendant is fine—it need not be a large, decorative ankh designed for hanging on a wall. Anubis is often depicted holding this symbol, and the energy that has built up around the godform makes the ankh an integral part of an assumption.

You might want an ankh, anyway. For nightkind, who try to connect with the unseen world, the ankh is another symbol worth wearing. It reminds us that our souls are eternal, and that there is a Dark God attributed to the time between incarnations. Coupled with the pentacle, which proclaims the importance of our spiritual development, the two symbols make a powerful pair to have on oneself.

The ankh you use in the rite should be placed on top of the personal item of the dead person you wish to reach. If you are not trying to make contact, simply put the ankh to the side of the altar that corresponds with your receiving hand.

With your altar set up, all that remains will be to wait until it's dark to begin, until psychic quiet time for best results (but you knew that by now).

The Anubis Rite

Cast a nocturnal circle through step twenty-four.

Pick up the ankh with your receiving hand.

Begin to go through the steps of godform assumption described in chapter 3. You should have a clear image of the God in your mind, from having either looked at the representation on your altar, or at any other statue or picture. Remember to only assume the human godform with jackal head.

For your spoken invocation, use the following (note that adding the line in parentheses is optional; do so only if you're trying to contact the deceased):

> *Gatekeeper of the Underworld, Lord Anubis, hear my call.*
> *Let your hand be the one to hold this ankh I now possess.*
> *Let your knowing eyes be the ones to gaze upon the portal before me,*
> *revealing the gates to the unseen.*
> *Let your alert ears be the ones to hear through this portal,*
> *imparting sounds from the Underworld.*
> *Be with me this night as I seek to know your realm.*
> *(Be with me this night as I seek contact with [name],*
> *whom you have guided to safety.)*
> *Be with me.*

As you say the last line, make your receiving arm rigid and extend it at a forty-five-degree angle so that the ankh is pointing at the altar.

Allow the form of Anubis to fully build, as described in chapter 3.

When you feel as one with the God, pass the ankh to your projecting hand.

Extend both arms so your hands are a few inches away from the nocturnal portal. Make a motion as if you are parting curtains or veils in front of the skrying device.

At this time, you may begin to skry and see if Anubis has any visions to share with you. If you have any particular questions that have been plaguing you about the afterlife, voice them now. The answers may come in a much stronger form than when you perform the technique of listening to the night.

You will find that in Anubis's presence you will feel somber yet energized. A quiet sort of confidence will come over you as you learn whatever you personally need to learn from this God. This part of the rite is entirely up to your desire and intuition—you need to determine what to ask of or seek from the God.

Anubis is a very precise God. He will grant you symbols and insights that answer, almost exactly, your queries about the afterlife. Do not expect to receive a lot of insights about things unrelated to such matters. It is his precise nature that will determine when you've had enough; you'll just know that Anubis has nothing more to offer on a subject at this time.

When you feel satisfied that the God is letting you know that he is done, close your eyes. You can go one of two ways at this point:

If you only desired time with the God, open your eyes, offer thanks to Anubis for coming, and let the godform dissipate as discussed in chapter 3. You can then put the ankh down and go on to close the circle.

If you wish to speak with the dead, however, continue with the following steps.

Open your eyes and look at the personal item of the deceased. Pick it up with your receiving hand. Touch it with the ankh you hold in your other hand.

Still looking at the object, try to remember what the person looked like (if you're not using a photo, spend a few minutes before the ritual refreshing your memory with a photo, if possible).

Say:

Anubis, I ask of you one more boon this night.
If (person's name) is still in the realm beyond, grant me sight to see (him or her).
If (name) has yet to move out of your reach, grant me the ability to hear
(his or her) voice.

Shift your gaze to the portal. Begin to repeat the deceased person's name. Let your voice slowly settle into a soft, almost chantlike whisper.

You may find yourself, in a few moments, communicating with the deceased as if through an open window.

Be prepared to make the most of what happens. Afterlife communication often only lasts anywhere from a few seconds to a minute or two. Anubis will control the length of the experience, as he is still invoked.

Use wisely whatever time you get with the deceased. That's all I can say about what will be a very personal experience for you.

When the vision ends, or if you do not receive one after about ten minutes or so, continue to thank Anubis (either way), and dissipate his form. Go on to close the circle.

Do not be discouraged if you can't contact a particular person. You might not be ready, or he or she might not be in the Summerland. The person might be in that realm, yet working out some issues first. Or he or she might have advanced from the Summerland to the higher realms, where you will one day rise to. Or, he or she might be on earth, working on doing what you're doing—trying to become one with the Source.

Regardless of what you do with it, the time you spend in the presence of Anubis will leave you much changed. Morbid as the idea may seem to others, invoking Anubis or other Underworld deities will make you enjoy life more—the world will seem to have much more meaning, and so, too, will what you plan on doing with your time here.

Conclusion

A New Beginning, Evolving in the Shadows

Ever notice how a candle seems to work with, not against, the darkness? It adds light to a room, sure, but doesn't really take away from the ambiance of the night. The darkness remains at the perimeter of the candle's light, embracing the energy—drawing the flame's emitted power into itself, in fact.

The candle is now lit.

You are ready to shine, ready to add your own powers to the night. This book has given you the basics you needed to change your life and to fully apply yourself to the Path of Night. You will never look out into the darkness the same way again.

Seek out the experiences that await you in that tangible blanket surrounding you each night. Move out into it, always able to find your way, always able to find out a little something extra.

More and more people each day are allowing themselves to openly accept the Craft. The Gods of Old are once again becoming vibrant, living godforms. The Gods of Night, in particular, are only beginning to regain some of their power that has lain dormant. But more and more nightkind are accepting the calling of these deities.

New and wondrous dark changes will be arising as the sun sets each night.

Use Nocturnal Witchcraft to strive for something more, and tap into the building energy around you.

Embrace the night.

Appendix A

Night's Gods and Goddesses

What follows is a list of Nocturnal Gods and Goddesses that I have invoked regularly. Most of these come from the three pantheons that I am most comfortable with—namely, Egyptian, Greek, and Sumerian. But there are a couple of godforms from other cultures included here as well.

This list is by no means exhaustive. Call upon those within it whom you can best relate to, but feel free to search for similar types of deities in other sources, too. In fact, the myths of the deities listed here are not thoroughly defined and described. I was intentionally vague in some ways to allow your own intuition a chance to fill in what the deities mean to you. I recommend that you read some mythology surrounding a deity of choice, as described in chapter 3.

Don't forget, of course, to also call upon the God and Goddess in universal forms. From time to time, no one name will feel just right.

Night Personified

Call on them for most types of nocturnal workings and thoughtforms, dream magick, and skrying or visualization help.

Hypnos: Greek God

His name is the Greek word for sleep, and the realms of sleep and dreams are his to command. It is likely that many ancient Greeks called on him for help with dream incubation, although he is also helpful with matters of receiving, in dreams, simple answers to questions. His mother is the ultimate embodiment of night in Greek mythology—Nyx.

Nephthys: Egyptian Goddess

She has been called upon to aid in rites of every basic type listed in these pages. The mother of Anubis and helper of all dark workings, she is a pure nocturnal deity, also encompassing some lunar, Underworld, and even protective aspects. Call on her for most anything after sunset.

Nyx: Greek Goddess

The mother of Hypnos, the Furies, and several other Gods, Nyx is the embodiment of nocturnal ether in all its forms. She is one of the first beings to emerge from Chaos, according to a creation myth. In the beginning there was night, indeed. If you call on a universal form of the Goddess of Night, you will be tapping into much of Nyx's energy. Seek her out for help with most anything in this book.

Dark Moon

Call on them for attuning with the Dark Moon, banishings, and any kind of positive but destructive magick, such as healing.

Hecate: Greek Goddess

This "Beloved of Zeus" is arguably one of the oldest deities known to the Greeks and, as a crone aspect, may essentially be the mother of the pantheon. Great power and wisdom abound in Hecate, and she is often considered the Goddess of Witchcraft. Use her intense magickal aid when you have serious needs. She is part of a triad of Goddesses (see Selene, Full Moon Goddess).

Morrigan: Celtic Goddess

Her symbols are the two related carrion birds, the crow and raven, either of which she often disguised herself as (more on crows and ravens in the *Gothic Grimoire*). Like the other Dark Moon Goddesses here, Morrigan is no typical crone, and one you may find yourself imagining being mature yet vibrant. She has reigned over battlefields when necessary, "destroying" the harmful effects of opposing armies. Morrigan can add fierce power to any banishing rite.

Pasht: Egyptian Goddess

This dark form of cat-headed Bast is associated with destructive magick. No crone, Pasht can bring the power of feline nimbleness and persistence to a Dark Moon rite, making your desired effect manifest regardless of the types of obstacles it encounters.

Full Moon

Call on them for attuning with the Full Moon, fertility, drawing things into your life, and for rites concerning energizing.

Nanna: Sumerian God

The father of Inanna, Nanna was often called the Lord of Wisdom. One of the few male lunar deities in the world, Nanna represents a unique perspective to rituals that feel somehow male, yet which clearly fall under the power of the Full Moon. Many pagans only associate the moon with female energy, but as with everything else there are male and female energies present. Imagine the different type of energy a God would bring to a lunar fertility rite, especially one for a man. Nanna can also be called in conjunction with his wife, Ningal, to have balanced polarity in a lunar rite.

Ningal: Sumerian Goddess

Inanna's mother and Nanna's wife. While she is far from being the most widely known Full Moon Goddess, Ningal is the Goddess I often feel drawn to when doing a Full Moon rite, likely because of my close personal connection with her daughter. As the Sumerian pantheon was called and worshiped within a dark magickal system, you may find that Ningal and the other Sumerian deities feel "right" to you, too.

Selene: Greek Goddess

As mentioned, Hecate is part of a triad of Goddesses (and not the only female triad in Greek mythology). For those who become comfortable working with crone Hecate, calling on mother Selene at the time of the Full Moon may seem natural. The maiden aspect, Diana, can be invoked in a rite that will be performed before the moon reaches Full, and Selene can then be called to finish such an increasing or drawing rite.

Protection

Call on them for protection, of course, but also for ensuring that karma keeps people in check when they deal with you.

Furies (Alecto, Megaera, and Tisiphone): Greek Goddesses

Another triad of Goddesses, these daughters of Nyx are known as the Angry Ones. Alecto can best protect against unseen enemies. Megaera should be called when you know someone is harboring ill will toward you. The most severe, Tisiphone can help you ensure that someone who wrongs you becomes fully aware of the consequences that the universe has in store (not consequences *you* send this person's way).

Kali: Indian Goddess

Describing the appearance of Kali is not easy. Most see her as something nightmarish, ranging from a fanged woman with four arms to such a figure with necklaces of skulls and blood upon her. Yet the harsh image is merely a representation of the role she takes on: that of a fierce protector. Call her only when you feel truly endangered.

Descent and Rebirth

Call on them for help in facing your own shadow self, approaching the unseen world, and obtaining wisdom.

Inanna (Ishtar and Astarte in later cultures): Sumerian Goddess

While archaeologists have argued as to why this beloved Goddess descended into the Underworld, it is clear that she managed to emerge even more powerful than when she entered. Despite being a multifaceted Goddess, Inanna can help you figure out how to handle most challenges from which you may need to emerge changed. Look into her myths to see the vast range of energies she also represents.

Khepera: Egyptian God

This beetle-headed God represented rebirth into a new existence. Call on his nocturnal form when you feel the need to let a part of yourself die so that a new part may be reborn. Wear a scarab beetle charm or ring to remind yourself of such an endeavor.

Kore/Persephone: Greek Goddess

Innocent Kore was dragged into the Underworld by Hades and eventually tricked into becoming his consort for part of each year—for what became the cold months. Upon the realization of her new role, she took on the name Persephone. Call on Kore when you feel blind to the effects of some forces in your life. Call on Persephone when you need guidance with a new part of your life that has begun and which you wish to control.

Underworld/Death

Call on them for an understanding of the afterlife, and for help in communicating with the dead.

Anubis: Egyptian God

As discussed in chapter 13, Anubis can help one achieve an understanding of the Underworld, in part because his godform has been called to provide just such aid in the past. His jackal eyes possess much wisdom, and through the loop in his ankh one can see eternity and the souls who live on.

Ereshkigal: Sumerian Goddess

As a darker aspect of a powerful Goddess, Ereshkigal reminds us that Death is not evil, but just another aspect of existence. Some of the melancholy nature of Death as a being comes through in her tale, for Ereshkigal did not choose her role. She was handed it, and must perform it to maintain the cosmic balance.

Hades/Thanatos: Greek God

Interestingly, Hades is described as ruling over an Underworld where the dead can either be in happiness (like the Summerland) or surrounded by lesson-teaching sorrows they've brought on themselves (the low realm). Invoke him to understand this aspect of the hereafter. To understand the process of moving on, you'd do better calling on Thanatos, who may very well be just another face of Hades, as Thanatos has been called the Lord of the Dead, and not just he who ushers them away.

Three Fates (Clotho, Lachesis, and Atropos): Greek Goddesses

The three fates symbolize the afterlife process that souls go through. Invoke them to learn about each phase of the process. Clotho creates our "life thread," or helps us pick the kind of life we need to enter. Lachesis measures the length of it, determining how many important challenges and learning experiences will come our way. Atropos cuts the life thread to carry us back to the afterlife when it is all over, making Atropos another type of traditional Death.

Appendix B

Nocturnal and Lunar Incense

Unless you find a scent that relates to a particular God or Goddess or pantheon (such as kyphi, which works well for all Egyptian deities), consider using one of the following incenses in your rites. They're broken up into two categories: The first consists of those scents that will aid most nocturnal workings (including invocations of deities of Night Personified, Protection, Descent and Rebirth, and the Underworld). The second set is incenses best suited for lunar rites (and invocations of Dark or Full Moon deities).

Note that for the Dark Moon rite itself (chapter 4), you would be better off using a nocturnal scent, as that particular rite is designed to reflect how the light of the moon has no sway on that particular night.

Nocturnal

Acacia gum
Amaranth
Ambergis

Balm of Gilead
Cinnamon
Clove
Cypress
Dittany of Crete
Dragon's Blood
Lily
Mastic gum
Mugwort
Patchouli
Pine
Poplar
Sage
Storax
Tamarisk
Tobacco
Vervain
Yew
Wisteria

Lunar

Camphor
Frankincense
Gardenia
Jasmine
Lemon
Lotus
Myrrh
Poppy seed
Rose
Sandalwood
Willow

Suggested Reading

Although there are no other books on Nocturnal Witchcraft as a tradition, some of these titles may supplement for you the techniques and teachings found in this book. If you're new to the Craft, a few books listed here will help you see more sides of the path before you decide to which tradition you'll devote your energies.

Achad, Frater. *Crystal Vision Through Crystal Gazing.* Chicago: Yogi Publication Society, 1923.

Bardon, Franz. *Initiation into Hermetics.* Wuppertal, West Germany: Dieter Ruggeberg Verlag, 1982.

Buckland, Raymond. *The Complete Book of Witchcraft.* St. Paul, Minn.: Llewellyn Publications, 1990.

Budge, E. A. Wallis. *The Egyptian Book of the Dead.* New York: Dover Publications, 1967.

Bullfinch, Thomas. *Bullfinch's Mythology.* New York: The Modern Library, 1998.

Cabot, Laurie. *Power of the Witch.* New York: Dell, 1989.

Conway, D. J. *Moon Magick: Myth & Magic, Crafts & Recipes, Rituals & Spells.* St. Paul, Minn.: Llewellyn Publications, 1995.

Cunningham, Scott. *Wicca: A Guide for the Solitary Practitioner.* St. Paul, Minn.: Llewellyn Publications, 1988.

Dalley, Stephanie. *Myths from Mesopotamia.* New York: Oxford University Press, 1989.

David-Neel, Alexandra. *Magic and Mystery in Tibet.* New York: University Books, 1958.

Dumont, Theron Q. *The Art and Science of Personal Magnetism.* Chicago: Yogi Publication Society, 1930.

Evans-Wentz, W. Y. *Tibetan Yoga and Secret Doctrines.* New York: Oxford University Press: 1958.

Fortune, Dion. *Through the Gates of Death.* London: The Aquarian Press, 1968.

Griffith, F., and Herbert Thompson. *The Leyden Papyrus.* New York: Dover Publications, 1974.

Konstantinos. *Contact the Other Side: 7 Methods for Afterlife Communication.* St. Paul, Minn.: Llewellyn Publications, 2001.

————. *Gothic Grimoire.* St. Paul, Minn.: Llewellyn Publications, 2002.

Leadbeater, C. W. *The Life After Death.* India: Theosophical Publishing House, 1952.

McCoy, Edain. *Magick & Rituals of the Moon.* St. Paul, Minn.: Llewellyn Publications, 1995.

Nelson, Robert A. *Hellstromism*. Alberta, Canada: Hades Publications, 1987.

Owen, Iris, and Margaret Sparrows. *Conjuring Up Philip: An Adventure in Psychokinesis*. New York: Harper & Row, 1976.

RavenWolf, Silver. *To Ride a Silver Broomstick*. St. Paul, Minn.: Llewellyn Publications, 1993.

Roderick, Timothy. *Dark Moon Mysteries: Wisdom, Power and Magic of the Shadow World*. St. Paul, Minn.: Llewellyn Publications, 1999.

Wendell, Leilah. *Encounters with Death: A Compendium of Anthropomorphic Personifications of Death from Historical to Present Day Phenomenon*. New Orleans: Westgate Press, 1996.

Wolkstein, Diane, and Samuel Noah Kramer. *Inanna: Queen of Heaven and Earth*. New York: Harper & Row, 1983.

Index

A Gothic Grimoire

Children of the night, take note—the dark tradition continues with *Gothic Grimoire*, the upcoming companion to *Nocturnal Witchcraft*. The nocturnal rites that comprise this dark grimoire are taken directly from Konstantinos' own Book of Shadows.

Celebrate your witchy ways with nocturnal rituals for the sabbats as well as the Dark and Full Moons. Explore advanced astral workings, including astral travel, creating thoughtforms, and banishing unwanted energies and entities. *Gothic Grimoire* includes the full text of the Inanna Rite of Opening the Gate, an advanced ritual for communication with the dead and entering the Underworld. For spellcraft ideas refer to the Nocturnicon, a codex of all things nocturnal, including spells and invocations for everything from attracting love, to improving night vision, to quitting a dangerous addiction.

Look for *Gothic Grimoire* soon at your favorite bookstore, or visit
www.llewellyn.com.

The Secret Tarots
Marco Nizzoli

As eternal as time, as deep as the sea, and as mysterious as fate itself, every card in *The Secret Tarots* has its own soul and a voice that whispers forgotten things to the hearts of all who will listen. Verging on the surreal, this sophisticated comic book style deck exemplifies many gothic ideals. One card is darkly angst-ridden while the next is playfully light. The deck is at once cutting-edge modern yet romantically historic—a symbolic representation of the enigmas we often find within ourselves. With images reminiscent of everything from Lord Byron to Mad Max, the ancient archetypes are dressed in new clothes. The great scope of time and experience is held together by Nizzoli's clean artistic style. All the pips are illustrated and all the cards are named in five languages: English, Italian, French, German, and Spanish. These seventy-eight cards represent the journey along an esoteric path leading to the understanding of secrets from the past, the present, and the future.

Boxed deck includes
78 full-color cards and 16-pp. fold-out instruction sheet
ISBN 0-7387-0021-5
$19.95 U.S. • $29.95 Can.